21 Days of Prayer for the Next Generation

STRATEGIC RENEWAL

Published by Strategic Renewal

www.strategicrenewal.com

Printed in the United States of America

ISBN 979-8-9926435-0-3

CONTENTS

FORWARD AND INVITATION

OVER 3,000 YEARS AGO, a shepherd boy who had become king of a nation proclaimed, *"One generation shall commend your works to another, and shall declare your mighty acts"* (Psalm 145:4). Over 2,000 years ago, a descendant of David, who is the King of Kings and humbly entered into human history, called twelve young adults saying, "Follow me, and I will make you fishers of men," (Matthew 4:19), and "You will see greater things than these...Truly truly I say to you, you will see heaven opened, and the angels of God ascending and descending on the Son of Man" (John 1:51).

You and I are here today, and you are holding this book because of the Father's faithfulness displayed through the generations. St. John Chrysostom once declared, "Let everything take second place to our care of our children, our bringing them up to the discipline and instruction of the Lord." We stand on the shoulders of preceding generations and carry the sacred privilege and responsibility to follow Jesus and "commend His work" to the next generation.

21 Days of Prayer for the Next Generation is a resource designed to equip you not only in how to pray, but also to encourage lifelong engagement with the next generation, so that we may continue to join the Lord's work in building His multi-generational Church. While some specifics are mentioned for our current younger generations (such as Gen Z and Gen Alpha), we believe the principles discussed will apply to many generations to come. The Lord has compiled a wonderful constellation of multigenerational authors to guide you over the next 21 days in Scripture-fed, Spirit-led, worship-based prayer for the next generation. After taking the time to slowly read through the Bible-based devotional, you are invited to pray along with the author of the chapter by accessing our library of audio prayers. Additionally, an appendix provides a worship-based prayer guide to help you pray more deeply as an individual, in a small group, or within your church.

Thank you for your willingness to invest the next 21 days in prayer for the next generation. We believe that your prayers will be seeds sown in the soil in the lives of students, young adults, and children that will bear lasting and God-glorifying fruit, "*that the next generation might know them [the glorious deeds of the Lord], the children yet unborn, and arise and tell them to their children, so that they should set their hope in God*" (Psalm 78:4, 6).

INTRODUCTION
WHY WE MUST FOCUS ON THE NEXT GENERATION

I REMEMBER LEARNING FROM a young age what is often titled "The Lord's Prayer." I used to recite it religiously on a daily basis. I even have tender memories of praying it with my dad at nighttime before going to bed, or whispering it under my breath while riding the bus to school. Yet when I was a young adult, the paradigm of my understanding of the Lord's Prayer was awakened. Rather than simply reciting it from time to time, it began to revolutionize my relationship with Jesus as it provided a rhythm of how to pray in the very same way Jesus did. It is indeed the foundational model of what we call Scripture-fed, Spirit-led, worship-based prayer. If that concept is new to you, this book will be a great introduction and guide!

Alongside reshaping the way I pray, the four rhythms of the Lord's Prayer have also greatly influenced why I believe we must focus on the next generation. Take a moment and slowly read Matthew's account of Jesus' model prayer in Matthew 6:9-13. Notice the personal plural pronouns. This not only emphasizes the priority of a corporate expression of prayer, but also, I believe, an experience of prayer that is multigenerational. From this paradigm, we have not only four movements of worship-based prayer, but also four reasons why we must focus on the next generation.

REASON 1: Looking Upward in Reverence...Because God Commands It!

As we look upward at who God is and how He has made Himself known to us in the Scriptures, we can see clearly what God focuses on. God's commands are a reflection of His character. Simply put, another way to explain why we should care about the next generation is that *God does.* We were all at one time in the category of the "next generation," and we are all here today because of the way others from preceding generations cared about us. In other words, we have all been recipients of the care and focus of older generations.

This is the way God has designed it. The very heart of heaven is multigenerational. God built deep care and focus on the next generation into the DNA of the family. God, as our Father, has adopted us in Christ to belong to a host of other spiritual brothers and sisters. In Christ, we have a familial obligation to care for and focus on discipling our younger siblings.

REASON 2: Looking Downward in Response...Because the Kingdom Depends on It!

How did God bring the kingdom of heaven to earth? He sent His beloved Son, Jesus, to build His church with a small bunch of ragamuffin young adults. In fact, Jesus Himself would be considered what we call today a next-generation leader. As He began his public ministry around the age of 30, we could even call him our Millennial Messiah!

It's interesting to note the age of the disciples that Jesus selected. His selection wasn't arbitrary, but divinely intentional. There's a lot of evidence that would lead us to conclude that Jesus' disciples were what we would categorize as "young adults."

First, most disciples were younger than their Rabbi, which would put the rest of the disciples at an age younger than 30. Secondly, in Jewish culture, a young man's discipleship training under a rabbi would usually begin between the ages of 13 and 15. If this pattern were consistent with the followers of Jesus, some of them may have joined Jesus as early as age 13 and would have still been teenagers at the time of His death, resurrection, and ascension.

Now, to be sure, God does not need anyone to accomplish His purposes. While He doesn't need us, He *wants* us. God, in His wisdom, set up life in a way that He gets more glory by involving us in the process of fulfilling His purposes. The same is true in the church today. The next generation doesn't just contain future leaders of the church; it also contains present leaders in the church. We must involve them in the church now to equip them for future leadership, and this is crucial because the kingdom depends on it.

REASON 3: Looking Inward...Because They Need It!

The statistics are sobering. According to a recent national study conducted by the Barna Research Group, only 10% of Christian twentysomethings have what they would call "resilient faith." Yet, as a millennial myself who has had the privilege of working and ministering closely with other millennials and Gen Z'ers, I can tell you they long for meaningful multigenerational connections. What better place to meet that need than through the local church?

One of the aspects I love most about the next generation is that they dream and believe big. Sometimes they can be a little overly idealistic, but it's inspiring! However, the next generation needs mentors to apply wisdom to their idealism. They also need models of worship that are a lifestyle and not just an event. Jesus didn't say to His disciples, "Come and listen to me," He said, "Follow me." You and I have a unique opportunity to invite a younger generation to follow us, as we follow Jesus (1 Corinthians 11:1).

REASON 4: Looking Outward...Because There's a Battle Waging For It!

A sobering reality is that there's someone else who's focused on the next generation as well, and his name is Satan. He is always seeking to thwart God's purposes, and one of his tactics is to inflict us with a generational myopia where we are consumed by self-focus. God's kingdom and church are beautifully diverse, and one of the expressions of that diversity is that of being multigenerational. Yet Satan seeks to silo the church in its neat and comfortable compartments. Satan wants to segregate, but the Holy Spirit wants to integrate.

So there's a battle waging...

The enemy is focused on the next generation and has schemes to steal, kill, and destroy. The next generation is literally clicking and scrolling their way into inclining rates of depression, anxiety, and suicide. The enemy has launched an onslaught of distraction, comparison, and compromise to the coming generation.

But Jesus has a plan, and a better one, too. I believe Jesus is raising up a remnant among the next generation who will be a part of ushering in spiritual awakening and revival in our land. You and I have an integral part to play as God calls, equips, empowers, and releases praying disciples and pastors with a laser-like focus and commitment to seek first the Kingdom of God above all else. This is not about hype or emotionalism; rather, I see a holy and humble hunger for the Lord in this next generation, and we can partner with Jesus in helping raise them up!

In fact, this is what Strategic Renewal is all about—equipping 6:4 pastors committed to prayer and word-powered ministry, encouraging 6:3 disciples marked by good reputation who are filled with the Spirit and wisdom, and who together are envisioning an awakening like we see in Acts 6:7. These next 21 days are designed to help you not only begin to notice and pray for the young people in your home, church, and community, but also to watch as the Lord opens up new opportunities to encourage, equip, and empower them toward their God-given purpose.

CHAPTER 1

SPIRITUAL FATHERS, MOTHERS, AND GRANDPARENTS

Thai Lam

> *Great is the LORD, and greatly to be praised, and his greatness is unsearchable. One generation shall commend your works to another, and shall declare your mighty acts. On the glorious splendor of your majesty, and on your wondrous works, I will meditate. They shall speak of the might of your awesome deeds, and I will declare your greatness. They shall pour forth the fame of your abundant goodness and shall sing aloud of your righteousness. (Psalm 145:3–7 ESV)*
>
> *Remember your leaders, those who spoke to you the word of God. Consider the outcome of their way of life, and imitate their faith. Jesus Christ is the same yesterday and today and forever. (Hebrews 13:7–8 ESV)*

As a father of three teenagers, I am constantly challenged by how my kids have a front-row seat as I talk about following Jesus and then endeavor to walk out my Christian faith daily. For better or worse, my kids witness the good examples, the bad habits, the godly moments, the leadership shortfalls, and the humbling apologies. But all in all, my hope is that as they hear my words and watch my life over the years and decades, they would see the goodness of God in a broken-but-redeemed man, who is clinging to Jesus and growing in a Godward life.

The same realities exist in the life of the church. Young disciples are watching the generations before them—how they love and trust God, how they treat strangers and family, what's most important in their lives, and so much more. These older and more seasoned saints have the opportunity to become spiritual mothers and fathers to the next generation if they would turn their hearts and open their lives to young people in their midst and testify of God's character, His ways, and His works as they have witnessed. Then, the next generation would have the chance to consider the outcome of the older generation's way of life and potentially imitate their faith.

> *For though you have countless guides in Christ, you do not have many fathers. For I became your father in Christ Jesus through the gospel. I urge you, then, be imitators of me. (1 Corinthians 4:15–16 ESV)*
>
> *You then, my child, be strengthened by the grace that is in Christ Jesus, and what you have heard from me in the presence of many witnesses entrust to faithful men, who will be able to teach others also. (2 Timothy 2:1–2 ESV)*

Today, young disciples have access to countless Christian podcasts, YouTube sermons and Sunday morning teachings that can be helpful tutors for their faith. But that is not the same as journeying with and being discipled by spiritual fathers and mothers in the faith.

Paul tells us that though we as believers can have many impactful teachers, we do not and cannot have many spiritual mothers and fathers. In a local church context, pastors may have many congregants that attend weekly, but they can only have a limited number of leaders that they are mentoring and investing in deeply.

Jesus taught crowds, ministered to individuals, and discipled twelve. If the Son of God had many followers but only twelve disciples, what does that say to us today? As much as we may desire to have greater Kingdom impact by reaching bigger crowds and more people, Jesus' leadership was different—He spent the minority of His time with the many and the majority of His time investing in a few. We, too, need to prioritize being spiritual fathers and mothers who are sowing into a few hungry, young disciples who in turn are maturing and growing into disciple makers. The next generation needs accessible and engaged spiritual fathers and mothers!

> *Behold, I will send you Elijah the prophet before the great and awesome day of the LORD comes. And he will turn the hearts of fathers to their children and the hearts of children to their fathers, lest I come and strike the land with a decree of utter destruction. (Malachi 4:5–6 ESV)*

> *And he will turn many of the children of Israel to the Lord their God, and he will go before him in the spirit and power of Elijah, to turn the hearts of the fathers to the children, and the disobedient to the wisdom of the just, to make ready for the Lord a people prepared. (Luke 1:16-17 ESV)*

In the last two verses of the Old Testament, the prophet Malachi prophesies about John the Baptist's forerunner ministry and warns us of the potential of judgment if the hearts of the older generation are not turned to the younger generation and the hearts of the young are not turned to the old. Additionally, the Gospel of Luke further highlights that John the Baptist would be used by the Lord to turn the hearts of fathers and mothers to sons and daughters as well as the "disobedient to the wisdom of the just" so that their generation would be prepared for the Lord's coming.

Today, there are more than 250 million college students on over 30,000 college campuses worldwide. What if pastors and churches globally were to turn their hearts in prayer towards thousands of students on college campuses down the street from their congregations? What if spiritual fathers and mothers were to turn their hearts and intercede for revival amongst sons and daughters in their communities, for the disobedient to turn to the wisdom of the just? And what if the older generation united in prayer with the younger generation for revival and spiritual awakening in their campuses, cities, and nation? What could God do and how might He respond? Let's find out!

— Pray for God to raise up spiritual mothers, fathers, grandparents, and pastors who would open and turn their hearts in prayer and discipleship towards the next generation.

— Pray for God to lead hungry young disciples to seasoned mothers and fathers who could mentor and invest in them.

— Pray for pastors and churches to gain God's heart and eyes for the thousands of college students who need Jesus on campuses down the street from their congregations.

Find a supplementary worship-based prayer guide to this chapter in the respective appendix.

Please, also, join us in prayer for this day through the SR App or at strategicrenewal.com/21days

CHAPTER 2

IDENTITY IN CHRIST—WHO DO YOU THINK YOU ARE?

Ricky Cassford

WHEN MY KIDS WERE younger, there was a day, not unlike many other days, where two of our four children were wrestling. My oldest son had pinned my oldest daughter down and was taunting her. With the clear upper hand, my son said, "Who do you think you are?!" To which my daughter, who was no more than seven years old at the time, in a small, relatively high-pitched but confident voice said, "I am a child of God!"

My son began to laugh at the unexpected comment, and we all enjoyed the truth out of the mouth of my baby girl. She had in fact given her life to Christ earlier that year. This moment has been a fond memory that has come up quite a few times, for our family, to this day.

Though this was an innocent game of sibling rivalry, it illustrates a great truth. There will be moments in everyday life where we feel pinned down by someone, or something, around us, and in those moments it is important to remember our identity; who we truly are.

Many of us look for our identity in things we can see, such as a job, a position, a title, a family name, a lifestyle, or even a diagnosis (be it mental or physical). While all of these things are a part of life, and some may even bring a certain amount of affirmation into our lives, it is not healthy for any of these things, in and of themselves, to be our identity. I would suggest that the character of an individual is far more important in describing who they are than these things.

Character has been described as, "the total quality of a person's behavior as shown by their habits, thoughts, and expressions." Everyone has a character of one kind or another, but the content of that character has to do with what a person truly believes. I would also suggest that this is the most important part of any individual in the eyes of God. So much so that God sent His Son to redeem the sinful character of the old you, and build into you a character more and more like Jesus. For anyone seeking to find their identity, whether in our generation or the next, the best place to look is Christ Jesus.

Second Corinthians 5:17 says, "Therefore, if anyone is in Christ, he is a new creation. The old has passed away; behold, the new has come."

The Truth About The Next Generation

Like anyone, the younger generation is looking for who they are. And remember, it will take time for them to find and solidify their identity, both in Christ and in the world of an ever-changing definition of adulthood, but they are on the hunt just like the rest of us. Even more important to remember is that once it is found, maintaining a healthy relationship with our God-given identity can still be difficult and full of temptation.

This even happened to Jesus in what you might call *The Testing of Jesus' Identity*. The Bible records a version of this situation in all three of the synoptic gospels, but most comprehensively in Matthew 4:1-11. Jesus endured this temptation to be able to specifically relate in this matter to you, me, and the next generation. In each specific test recorded, He faced an adversary that was questioning His identity: "If you are the Son of God..." (v.3&6) and "...if you will...(act out of character to who you are)" (v.9).

Like us, Jesus faced three common areas in the testing of His identity. The apostle John describes them as *Desires of the Flesh, The Pride of Life,* and *Desires of the Eyes (1 John 2:16).* These same basic temptations have been around since the initial temptation in the garden (see Genesis 3:6). It seems our adversary doesn't have any new tricks!

As recorded in Matthew 4, Jesus was tempted to deny who He was and to give in to the *desire of the flesh* by the suggestion that He use His power inappropriately to make bread (v.3). Jesus was tempted to deny who He was and to give in to the *pride of life* by foolishly claiming a promise, out of context, for holy protection (vv.5-6). Jesus was tempted to deny who He was and to give in to the *desire of the eyes* by taking up a deceitful shortcut in God's path, when God had already planned to give Him those very things (v.9).

These things are common pitfalls for all of us, but especially for those who have not solidified their identity in Christ. *But this is our ministry as Christians:* the ministry of reconciliation. Second Corinthians 5:17-20 reminds us that we are His ambassadors. The next generation needs, and wants, someone authentic and accurate to believe in. This is why the term ambassador for Christ is so appropriate. Authentically informing, explaining, and even appropriately exhorting the next generation that this identity is waiting for them is so important as we tell them the Lord's glorious deeds, His might, and the wonders that He has done (Psalm 78:4).

So, in your prayers for the next generation, keep on your intercessory list their character concerning desires of the flesh, desires of the eyes, and the pride of life, while seeking how you might actively be an ambassador for Christ and His desire for them to find their identity in Him.

Find a supplementary worship-based prayer guide to this chapter in the respective appendix.

Please, also, join us in prayer for this day through the SR App or at strategicrenewal.com/21days

---

CHAPTER 3

PURPOSE AND CALLING

Justin Jeppesen

"WHAT DO YOU WANT to be when you grow up?" That age-old question seemed to ring afresh in my ears as I overheard my eight-year-old son ask my six-year-old daughter. As their little voices gave words to their expansive imaginations, I began to ponder how I've been asked that same question countless times. The desire to ask and answer such a question finds its source in Divine design. Wired deep within the human soul is a longing to know, "Why am I here?" And how we answer this critical question maps the course of the lives we live and the legacy we leave behind. Yet in each generation, the question of one's purpose and calling holds a central role and is often met by confusion, insecurity, and mystery.

If there was anyone who had resolute clarity and conviction about their purpose and calling, it was Jesus of Nazareth. Before His miraculous birth, the angel of the Lord announced to Joseph that his son, conceived by the Holy Spirit in Mary, should be called Jesus, "for he will save his people from their sins" (Matt. 1:21). Just 12 years later, the youth-group-aged Jesus, who had recently been accidentally left behind in Jerusalem, was found in the temple and declared to His perplexed and worried mother, "Why were you looking for me? Did you not know that I must be about my Father's business?" (Luke 2:49). Then, some 18 years later, on the heels of a 40-day fast in the wilderness and overcoming the devil's temptations, Jesus went public with His purpose when He declared that He was the fulfillment of Isaiah's prophecy to proclaim "good news to the poor"..."liberty to the captives...", and "the year of the Lord's favor" (Luke 4:18-19).

Additionally, Jesus would go on to declare His calling, saying things like, "The Son of Man came not to be served but to serve, and to give his life as a ransom for many" (Mark 10:45). And "For this purpose I was born and for this purpose I have come into the world—to bear witness to the truth" (John 18:37). Then, after His sacrificial death and victorious resurrection, Jesus proclaimed to His fearful and insecure disciples, "As the Father has sent me, even so I am sending you" (John 20:21). From the life and ministry of Jesus, we can draw a wealth of wisdom and rich application for how we can pray for the next generation around their purpose and calling.

Purpose is Rooted in a Personal Relationship

Often, the question of one's calling and purpose is elevated to the highest importance. However, this question is actually downstream from the most ultimate question, which is, "Who is God?" This question is the headwaters or foundation from which all of life flows and is built. For example, consider how Jesus' calling was an overflow of decades of cultivated intimacy with His heavenly Father. He essentially spent 30 years preparing for the three years that He would publicly accomplish His purpose. This is why He would often steal away before the waking hours of the day to spend passionate and uninterrupted time with His Father in heaven (Mark 1:35).

Pray that the next generation would recognize that their first and primary calling is to intimacy with Jesus, which would lead to the fulfillment of the Father's purposes in and through them. Pray for sensitive souls to the Good Shepherd's voice and for courageous obedience to follow wherever He leads. Ultimately, our purpose is not something we achieve or produce, but is something that is discovered and received through abiding in Christ.

Calling is Confirmed in Community

While every Christian has a general and primary call to be rooted in a personal relationship with Christ, our Creator has uniquely wired us with specific aptitudes, desires, and gifts. Yet our personal relationship with Jesus is not merely individual but communal. Each of us is a member of Christ's body and has been equipped to serve vocationally and sacrificially with love and joy. It's been said that our calling is clarified at the intersection of our greatest passion with the world's deepest need. And as God's masterpieces created in Christ, He has prepared good works for us to walk in that flow from the unique way He made us (Ephesians 2:10).

When we pray for the next generation, let us petition the Father to help young men and women discover their place of belonging and service in the local church, and also to reveal their unique gifts that reflect God's glory to their community, city, and world.

Focus on Being before Doing

It is wise to be cautious about reducing our purpose and calling to mere activity or the mastering of certain competencies. Because our first call is one of relational intimacy, it is a matter of being before doing. Rather than asking the perennial question, "*What* do you want to be when you grow up?" which emphasizes doing over being, we ought to begin asking, "*Who* do you want to become when you grow up?" When we focus on forging character rather than developing a career, a Christ-centered contentment and fruitfulness will ensue, regardless of the role, vocation, or assignment the Lord entrusts to us.

So when we pray for the next generation, let's always consider the example of Christ so that their purpose and calling will also be rooted in "being about the Father's business," and always adorn the gospel of the Kingdom.

Find a supplementary worship-based prayer guide to this chapter in the respective appendix.

Please, also, join us in prayer for this day through the SR App or at strategicrenewal.com/21days

---

CHAPTER 4

HOLINESS IN A HOSTILE CULTURE

Dennis Henderson

EARLY IN THE BIBLE, one finds accounts of those who followed the one true God who faced an inimical culture. The nation of Israel faced battles that were more than military skirmishes. They involved protecting their spiritual and moral values, which were given to them by God. Those who committed to following Jesus in the New Testament writings faced persecution, suffering, and even death in a hostile world. As a Christ follower today, it should not be shocking to you to sense that you are faced daily with a culture that opposes the very core of Scripture's teachings, whether it is the conversations around you, the professor in college, the media, or advertising that desires to seduce you to an immoral life. In reality, the battle is more than just a moral code; it is the rule of God in this world. Ephesians 6:12 reminds us of the war we face. "For we do not wrestle against flesh and blood, but against the rulers, against the authorities, against the cosmic powers over this present darkness, against the spiritual forces of evil in the heavenly places." This is our reality today. It is a battle beyond ideologies. It is truly an encounter with the prince of darkness who hates everything good, true, and holy.

Holiness, in simple and practical terms, is living a life that is built on the teachings of Scripture, which at its core is to reflect the life of Jesus and the biblical truths to those around you. It is not a combative life, and yet it is not a life of retreat. It is marked by love, compassion, purity, and the desire to point people to the message of the gospel. It is about living intentionally in a manner that reflects God's character.

Holiness is not living in isolation on a hillside with a group of monks. Jesus taught in John 17:14-16, " I have given them your word, and the world has hated them because they are not of the world, just as I am not of the world. I do not ask that you take them out of the world, but that you keep them from the evil one. They are not of the world, just as I am not of the world." He instructed us not to live a life of isolation, but a life of penetration. We are to be in the world, but not of it. We are like a boat that does well as it floats on the water. However, if the water gets into the boat, then there is a danger of the boat sinking.

We live in a world that overtly and subjectively challenges us through relativism, distractions, and temptations that appeal to our flesh. It desires to mock the teachings of biblical morality and marginalize those of faith. It appears to be enhanced more than any generation before us through the screens of television and theater, as well as the multiple social media platforms. The words of John are greatly needed as he tells us not to love the world or any of its attractions of pleasure, possessions, or desired power. "Do not love the world or the things in the world. If anyone loves the world, the love of the Father is not in him. For all that is in the world—the desires of the flesh and the desires of the eyes and pride of life—is not from the Father but is from the world. And the world is passing away along with its desires, but whoever does the will of God abides forever" (1 John 2:15) Peter joins in with John, reminding us that there is a war against our souls, but also tells us that a day of judgment is coming. Thus, we keep an eternal perspective in the midst of this corrupt world. "Beloved, I urge you as sojourners and exiles to abstain from the passions of the flesh, which wage war against your soul. Keep your conduct among the Gentiles honorable, so that when they speak against you as evildoers, they may see your good deeds and glorify God on the day of visitation" (1 Peter 2:11). With these truths in mind, we strive to embody the words of Jesus in Matthew 5:13-16, to be salt and light in this world.

With words of instructions, we ground our lives in humility, discernment, and grace, and call upon our God, beginning with worship of Him and His work in our lives. We bow to Him as our most prized possession, who is worthy of every effort and sacrifice we make. When we lean into Him for our dependency, whatever surrounds us with opposition dims in light of Christ's amazing love and ability to rescue us when needed. Daily, we pray for not our will, but His, to be done in our lives. Every generation has faced the hostility of the world; thus, in the chaos of what surrounds us, we draw from His presence in our lives. The Holy Spirit is our comforter, our teacher, and our empowerment to live a life of holiness in a world that Jesus said would be filled with trouble. " I have said these things to you, that in me you may have peace. In the world, you will have tribulation. But take heart; I have overcome the world" (John 16:33).

As you pray today for the next generation, thank God that He has not left you alone in this chaotic world. Surrender to live a life of holiness and purpose. Then ask the holy God who lives in you to give wisdom, grace, and peace to love a world that needs your Savior.

Find a supplementary worship-based prayer guide to this chapter in the respective appendix.

Please, also, join us in prayer for this day through the SR App or at strategicrenewal.com/21days

---

CHAPTER 5

DEVELOPING PRAYING LEADERS

Drew Humphrey

> *"And he was teaching them and saying to them, 'Is it not written, "My house shall be called a house of prayer for all the nations"?' " Mark 11:17 (ESV)*

Most ministers know how to recruit, train, and release various types of ministry teams—leadership teams, serve teams, small group leaders, mission teams, worship teams, even coffee teams. In fact, if a leader cannot build and release teams, their ability to extend the Gospel's impact will be severely limited.

But here is a vital question to reflect on: Am I training and raising up teams of prayer leaders, in addition to all the others I equip?

If not, why is that?

The 19th-century prayer leader E.M. Bounds once wrote:

> *"Where are the Christlike leaders who can teach the modern saints how to pray? Do our leaders know we are raising up a prayerless set of saints? Let them (the leaders) come to the front and do the work, and it will be the greatest work that can be done."*

God's Highest Purpose For His Church

What would you say is God's highest purpose for your ministry or church? You might answer with:

1. **Matthew 16:13–19** – Confessing that Jesus is Savior.
2. **Matthew 28:18–20** – Making disciples of all nations, baptizing, and teaching.
3. **Acts 1:8** – Being filled with the Spirit and serving as Christ's witnesses.

While each of these is biblical and essential, are they the highest purpose? Remember the verse at the start of this chapter: *"My house shall be called a house of prayer."*

As David Butts put it in his incredible book on prayer *Forgotten Power*:

> *"The owner of the house gets to nickname the house, and God has nicknamed His house the House of Prayer."*

God could have chosen to call it a house of preaching, worship, evangelism, discipleship, or church planting. But He chose *prayer*. This doesn't diminish the importance of those other functions, but it does highlight something we often miss: much of our leadership training, strategies, and next-generation equipping does not prioritize prayer.

In fact, many of us do everything else long before we dedicate extended time to prayer—or before we intentionally teach others how to pray.

As spiritual parents, brothers, and sisters to the next generation, we cannot neglect the responsibility of developing praying leaders. If we fail to train them in prayer, we unintentionally train them in self-sufficiency and copy-cat ministry models—approaches that rely on human strength rather than the power of Heaven.

How Do We Develop Praying Leaders?

1. **Model Prayer Personally.**

   The heart of the leader must be deeply rooted in prayer. Romans 2:21 asks, *"You then who teach others, do you not teach yourself?"* We cannot raise up praying leaders if we ourselves are not convinced that prayer matters.

   A prayerless life is the closest a Believer comes to atheism. Without prayer, we are silently declaring that we don't need God's help.

   So, leader, reorient your daily rhythm around prayer. Serious prayer. Pray in the morning and evening. Pray while driving. When counseling someone over coffee, spend more time seeking God's wisdom than offering recycled advice filled with cliches. In team meetings, dedicate a significant portion of the time to prayer, not just planning.

2. **Create Rhythms of Prayer For Others Who Follow You.**

   What prayer rhythms are you modeling and inviting others into?

a) In worship gatherings, is prayer just a transition between songs or is it a key element of why you are together?
b) Could you take five minutes from a service to form prayer huddles around specific needs? Instead of singing a fifth song, maybe you sing four songs and fill that open slot with these prayer circles.
c) Do you activate prayer teams and prayer altars that encourage genuine intercession during your gatherings?

If someone snuck into the back of the weekly ministry that you lead, what are the odds—in minutes—that they would catch your group praying? I think that number is pretty small for most of us.

What types of weekly, rhythmic prayer groups do you lead and promote? A decade ago, our church had 15 men at an 8am weekly Sunday prayer gathering. Today, 125 men meet weekly—and most are under 23 years old! That didn't just accidentally happen; it took intention, teaching, and invitations over the long haul.

But don't limit prayer to church walls. We need to fall in love with living room prayer meetings again—families, friends, and neighbors coming together to be activated in prayer.

3. **Teach Them That Prayer Is Service.**

Prayer is not only communion with God; it is active service in His Kingdom. When we pray, we intercede for others, call on God's protection, and ask for His wisdom. And more!

Prayer isn't meant to be some passive, lifeless activity for only a few in the church. No, prayer is meant to be full of zeal, calling upon the Living God in Heaven as we depend upon Him for all of the needs in our lives, for all of the days of our lives.

It has been said before that people of prayer are the rescuers of the Church from its material tendencies. They pour into it the original spiritual forces, lift it off the sandbars of materialism, and press it out into the ocean depths of spiritual power.

Let's do our part. And let's train the next generation to continue in the important work of prayer.

Find a supplementary worship-based prayer guide to this chapter in the respective appendix.

Please, also, join us in prayer for this day through the SR App or at strategicrenewal.com/21days

---

CHAPTER 6

GOSPEL PARTNERSHIPS

Justin Jeppesen

> *I thank my God in all my remembrance of you, always in every prayer of mine for you all making my prayer with joy, because of your partnership in the gospel from the first day until now. And I am sure of this, that he who began a good work in you will bring it to completion at the day of Jesus Christ. (Philippians 1:3-6)*

There's an old adage that succinctly states, "none of us is any better than all of us." Similarly, there is an African proverb that proclaims, "If you want to go fast, go alone. But if you want to go far, go together." These statements have obvious broad applications to areas such as team sports, choirs, organizational staff, and similar groups. Yet this proverbial statement speaks to the deep reality written within the human heart: the desire to be intimately connected and experience a shared life with others.

More importantly, there's a word and concept that's woven through the storyline of the Scriptures that describes the remarkable communal life of the Church. It's the word *koinonia,* which often gets translated to fellowship, sharing, association, or partnership. It carries the idea of a close relationship involving common interests and a united purpose. Not only is this rich word a reality because of the gospel, it is also a means by which the gospel is advanced. From one generation to another, God's kingdom expands through partnership.

A Thankful Reminder

If ever there was a man who had the personality, giftedness, experience, and charisma to make it on his own, it was the Apostle Paul. Yet as he wrote from prison, this ancient pastor was filled with thanksgiving when he remembered the Philippian church that had generously and sacrificially supported him as he sought to bring the gospel to the ends of the earth. Indeed, Paul was completely dependent on God, yet God's provision also comes through an interdependence within Christ's body, the Church.

As we pray for the next generation, may we, like Paul, express our gratitude and joy for the younger members of Christ's body. Pray for a growing mutual and multi-generational gratitude to permeate the Church so that the variety of generations would not view themselves as competitors but as partners.

Prayerful Partnership

When we live in intimate connection with God and others towards a common mission, it not only produces thanksgiving and joy, it also renews our vision. We move from an individualistic mindset to a communal one. We recognize that we cannot accomplish Kingdom purposes through worldly means. Christendom has had its fair share of fragmentations and fiefdoms. And perhaps now more than ever, the next generation is looking for gospel partnerships. They are seeking true partnerships over partisanship, and cities over silos. In other words, they long to be a part of a genuine move of

God, and to participate in a purpose that exceeds their own imagination and eclipses their own expectations. This is possible through the multi-generational Church, living in prayer partnerships with other churches, parachurch ministries, and like-minded missional organizations.

Church, may we pray fervently for the Lord to connect the dots between churches, communities, and ministries. God's mission is way bigger than any one denomination, initiative, or movement. Pray for God to use the next generation to lead the way for gospel partnerships to unite together so that God's good work would be generated and sustained by the Spirit's power.

Brought to Completion

There is another old adage that emerged among the early Church fathers, making the bold claim that "Without God, we cannot; without us, God will not." While each of us has a significant role in advancing the good news so that nations are discipled, we must remember that God is the one who begins and completes His good work. Therefore, the work we do is not something we do *for* God but *with* God. It's not that our Sovereign Lord needs us, but that He wants us, and desires us to work together in partnership with Him. What an amazing reality!

As Paul declares in Philippians 1:6, we can have the assurance that God *always* finishes what He starts. So may we pray for that assurance in God's work in, with, and through the next generation. Pray for new work to begin in young people across our churches, communities, cities, and countries. Pray that the next generation will live with the end in view, that "the day of Jesus Christ" would compel them to be faithful towards the completion of God's good work that He began in them.

In the summer of 1806, five college students gathered in a field to pray for world missions. While they were praying, a thunderstorm arose. Undeterred by inclement weather, they sought shelter underneath a haystack and persisted in prayer for the spread of the gospel around the world. Their passion and partnership led to the establishment of the American Board of Commissioners for Global Missions, which would eventually mobilize hundreds of missionaries across Asia, Africa, and the Pacific Islands. This Haystack Revival at Williams College in Massachusetts also became known as the Student Volunteer Movement, inspiring gospel partnerships across numerous universities such as Yale and Princeton. Remarkably, historians estimate that nearly half of the populations in some of these colleges committed themselves to missionary and evangelistic work during this period.

May the Lord, through our prayers for the next generation, multiply these good works, such as the Haystack Prayer Meeting, in our day all over again!

Find a supplementary worship-based prayer guide to this chapter in the respective appendix.

Please, also, join us in prayer for this day through the SR App or at strategicrenewal.com/21days

---

CHAPTER 7

LEGACY-MINDED CHURCHES

Daniel Henderson

EVERY CHURCH, REGARDLESS OF its size, history, or location, faces a pressing question: What kind of legacy will we leave for future generations? While buildings, budgets, and programs may endure for a season, the true legacy of a local church is measured by the faithfulness of its discipleship, especially in how it invests in the next generation of believers.

At Strategic Renewal, we believe deeply that the future of the church depends on leaders and congregations who are committed to being legacy-minded. This means more than simply maintaining ministries or preserving traditions. It requires a Spirit-led conviction to pass on a vibrant, biblical faith to our sons and daughters, our students, and the young leaders God is raising up in our midst.

A Biblical Mandate for Legacy

The call to discipleship is not optional. From Genesis to Revelation, Scripture reveals God's heart for generational impact. In Deuteronomy 6, God commands His people to diligently teach His words to their children—talking about them at home, on the road, in the morning, and at night. The psalmist declares, "We will not hide them from their children, but tell to the coming generation the glorious deeds of the Lord, and his might, and the wonders that he has done" (Psalm 78:4).

Jesus Himself, before ascending to the Father, gave His disciples the Great Commission: *"Go therefore and make disciples of all nations"* (Matthew 28:19). Implicit in this command is generational transfer—disciples who make disciples, who then disciple others. Paul embodied this when he told Timothy, *"The things you have heard me say... entrust to reliable people who will also be qualified to teach others"* (2 Timothy 2:2).

The biblical picture is clear: healthy churches do not exist for themselves but for those who will come after them. A church that neglects discipleship of the next generation risks becoming a monument to the past rather than a movement into the future.

The Crisis of Neglect

We cannot ignore the reality before us. Stories of evangelistic movements on college campuses are becoming more common. Yet, in most cases, this is not translating into church attendance. Some have described this problem as "revival and retreat" as young people are absent from the church in alarming numbers. Many graduate from high school and graduate from the church at the same time. Too often, they have not experienced authentic, relational discipleship within the body of Christ.

Instead, churches can fall into the trap of entertaining youth rather than equipping them. Programs replace relationships. Events replace mentoring. The result is a fragile faith that struggles to withstand the cultural pressures of a secularized world.

If we are not intentional about discipleship, we should not be surprised when the next generation does not carry the torch of faith. The church's legacy cannot be left to chance.

A Call to Spirit-Led Renewal

What, then, must we do? The answer is not found in bigger buildings or more polished programs. The answer is renewal—Scripture-fed, Spirit-led, worship-based renewal that prioritizes prayer and discipleship.

Churches that are legacy-minded must cultivate a culture of prayer that permeates every level of ministry. When young people see their parents, pastors, and mentors crying out to God, depending on His Spirit, and anchoring their lives in His Word, they encounter authentic Christianity. They see faith not as a ritual but as a relationship.

From this culture of prayer flows intentional discipleship. Older believers invest in younger ones. Parents are equipped to disciple their children. Pastors prioritize developing young leaders. Congregations celebrate the work of God in the lives of their students and release them to serve.

Practical Pathways to Legacy

How can churches begin to live this out? Let me suggest a few practical steps:

1. **Prioritize intergenerational prayer.** Create spaces where young and old pray together. Let students hear the wisdom of seasoned saints and allow the faith of the young to inspire fresh passion in adults.

2. **Equip parents.** The primary responsibility for discipleship lies in the home. Churches must provide resources, encour-

agement, and accountability to help parents lead their children spiritually.

3. **Invest in mentoring.** Every young believer should have a Paul and a Timothy—someone discipling them and someone they are discipling. The church must cultivate this chain of investment.

4. **Empower young leaders.** Give students real opportunities to serve and lead. Don't wait until they are adults to entrust them with responsibility. The best way to train the next generation is to involve them now.

5. **Keep the gospel central.** Ultimately, our legacy is not about us—it is about Christ. Everything we teach and model must point to the finished work of Jesus and the transforming power of His Spirit.

A Vision Worth Pursuing

When a church becomes legacy-minded, it sees beyond the next program, budget, or building project. It begins to dream about the lives of children yet unborn who will walk in the ways of the Lord because of today's faithfulness.

Imagine a church where grandparents, parents, and children worship together, united in prayer and purpose. Imagine students who, rather than drifting from the faith, are equipped to stand boldly for Christ in their schools, workplaces, and communities. Imagine young leaders rising up, trained and empowered by older saints who poured into them.

This is not a dream beyond our reach. It is the very design of God for His church. But it requires intentionality, sacrifice, and above all, a reliance on the Spirit of God.

Conclusion

The choice before us is urgent. We can continue with business as usual, hoping that the next generation will somehow catch the faith by osmosis. Or we can heed the biblical call to be legacy-minded, discipling our young people with passion, prayer, and perseverance.

The future of the church depends on it. Our children and grandchildren are worth it. And the glory of Christ demands it.

May God grant us the courage to leave a legacy that echoes into eternity.

Find a supplementary worship-based prayer guide to this chapter in the respective appendix.

Please, also, join us in prayer for this day through the SR App or at strategicrenewal.com/21days

---

CHAPTER 8

AUTHENTIC RELATIONSHIPS

Ricky Cassford

WHEN THE PRESIDENT OF the United States ordered the nation to stay home, the fine-dining restaurant at which I worked had to close its doors for the foreseeable future, and I lost my job. However, the Lord provided an immediate full-time position at a home improvement warehouse that had previously employed me in a part-time capacity. This, in turn, eventually led to my meeting a young man who had not yet turned 20. I myself was well into my forties, but for some reason, this young man took a liking to me. I once had a Youth Pastor say to his volunteers, of which I was one, that kids today live in a world that pays no attention to them, and they are so desperate to be heard, that simply listening to them is an act they consider love. This young man was no different. The connection that was created between me and this young man was affected by this thought, and because of it, I recognized his need for validation and his desire to be heard. He was looking for an authentic relationship. The relationship that we formed has lasted to this day, even through some pretty rocky moments over the years, including major depression, suicidal thoughts, 3:00 am phone calls, and an interstate relocation to find himself through occupations questionable to my Christian standards. He recently said to me that I was THE guy in his life that he could always turn to, no matter what he had done.

The consequence of this young man's authenticity was my compassion, acceptance, and willingness to relate to a genuine heart that had been led astray by the glitz and glamor of this world that has no ability to satisfy. I'd been there. He and I have had many straight-talk conversations about God and His love, but also about God's standards, even though he did not claim any religion besides a cultural Judaism at the time. Authenticity breeds authenticity. He could clearly see that I loved and cared for him through the unconditional manner in which I interacted with him, and so when I authentically expressed my concerns based on God's desires for his life, he was far more willing to listen because his basic need, authentic love, had been met.

An authentic relationship is not one that allows honesty about disobedience or sin to be dismissed out of hand, nor is it one that is at risk of dissolution because of the other party's past (even a very present past) if any given line is crossed in their life or behavior.

Ephesians 4:29-32

> *"Let no corrupting talk come out of your mouths, but only such as is good for building up, as fits the occasion, that it may give grace to those who hear. And do not grieve the Holy Spirit of God, by whom you were sealed for the day of redemption. Let all bitterness and wrath and anger and clamor and slander be put away from you, along with all malice. Be kind to one another, tenderhearted, forgiving one another, as God in Christ forgave you."*

Unfortunately, my family has experienced, to our collective chagrin, another type of consequence for authenticity. As much as we would all like authentic relationships, and it seems that the church should produce those who readily engage in them, this is not always the case. Under God's sovereignty, and carried by His grace through these instances, we have faced a number of inauthentic relationships looking down their noses at us, as if a thing confessed could never even have been considered by them or any other "good Christian." Though this is a poor response to someone's authenticity, we have probably all experienced something similar.

Does this mean that we don't expect one another to live up to a standard of righteousness? At the risk of sounding like Paul, by no means! But neither does it mean that we allow their failure to achieve that standard to be a reason to act as if we have never failed ourselves, or to be disingenuous in our relation to them.

None of us does what we think we ought to do, which makes us all hypocrites. Even those outside of the family of God each have an idea of how life should be led, and none of them do it the way they think it should be done either. We cannot do what we think/know that we should do. This is the reason Jesus came to forgive our debt that we could not pay! Many in the next generation, even many outside the church, seem to value honesty in this respect, especially when it comes to relationships. They actually seem to embrace the messy, as long as there is genuine love.

A recent blog from one of my graphics vendors was titled, "Perfect is Dead - Learn Why Raw Content is Getting More Attention." The article was about how most consumers of media today are more likely to relate to a video presentation that looks less polished because it reminds them that real life is not lived flawlessly. This, even in itself, seems to be indicative of a desire in the next generation for authenticity. We can all learn from this God-honoring perspective on relationships, and be authentic with one another, and full of grace when others are with us.

A Matter of Timeline

Keeping authentic relationships, especially with those in the next generation, seems to be a balance of expecting the best and gracefully forgiving them. I have recently thought about it this way, and the above Scripture seems to say the same: if sin has occurred (notice the past tense), then an authentic relationship would freely offer forgiveness knowing 1) that they too have sinned, 2) that they themselves are capable of any sin—but by the grace of God, and 3) that they too have been forgiven.

But equally so, if a friend is seeking to make a decision on something (notice the present tense) that could lead them into disobedience or sin, then an authentic relationship would 1) share with them what God's desire is in that circumstance, 2) pray with them from their heart, and 3) exhort them to make the most God-honoring decision. And yet, as most pastors know, it is one of the most disheartening things in ministry that people don't always do as you have exhorted them, only to then find themselves in a difficult situation. This moves the particular instance from the present tense example to the past tense example, remembering that our job is not to change them or shame them into righteousness, but to authentically love them as Christ loved us when we didn't do what He asked us.

While authenticity may be received differently, and we can't predict who will respond in which way, God wants us to be in authentic relationships with each other, treating each other genuinely as Paul described in Ephesians 4—tenderhearted, and forgiving one another.

Find a supplementary worship-based prayer guide to this chapter in the respective appendix.

Please, also, join us in prayer for this day through the SR App or at strategicrenewal.com/21days

---

CHAPTER 9

LONELINESS, DEPRESSION, AND ANXIETY

Angela Lam

WHILE HEAVILY DISTRACTED and overstimulated, young people overlook the ache of loneliness in their hearts. Despite the ache being deep and real, they often turn to busyness or ambition, skipping all the cues for genuine connection, first with God, and second with godly community. Posting something on social media replaces a true reaching out to those around them. And massive gaming stimulation robs their mind of looking further for interaction with the Holy Spirit and the Word, leaving them disillusioned by the actual lack of their efforts and still alone.

As grown adults and leaders, we too are susceptible to the void-covering, empty satisfaction media and other distractions offer us. It may look different for us, but we can relate to the truth that a life-giving connection can't be made through superficial acts and outlets. And that gives us the exact direction and empathy needed to intercede for the hearts of this young generation.

Left unacknowledged and overlooked, the need for connection surpasses loneliness and can lead to depression. Comparison, seeing others' accomplishments or level of influence online, gives an awful—sometimes deafening—sense that others are forging ahead while the observer is left behind. Loneliness is no longer a subtle burden in their hearts but is leading to depression. Hours of wasted time pass. Days of low energy and little desire slip into weeks. And thoughts of the future are replaced with the raw survival question, "Why do I even need to get out of bed?"

Anxiety creeps in, causing neurological responses of fight, flight, or freeze to surface: the fight to anxiously keep busy, distracted, and stimulated; the defensive flight to move and assume that where they are is the problem; or the imprisoning freeze of second-guessing and crippling uncertainty.

The reality of loneliness may have been, by design, a hunger to push us towards life-giving connection. And the many temptations that seem to offer relief are relatable to the temptations Jesus encountered while alone in the wilderness. It's not written that Jesus was explicitly lonely or anxious, but after 40 days, Satan chose to tempt Jesus the way he tempts and pursues many in today's lonely generation.

Matthew 4:1-11 reads: "Then Jesus was led by the Spirit into the wilderness to be tempted by the devil. After fasting forty days and forty nights, he was hungry. The tempter came to him and said, 'If you are the Son of God, tell these stones to become bread.' Jesus answered, 'It is written: "Man shall not live on bread alone, but on every word that comes from the mouth of God".' Then the devil took him to the holy city and had him stand on the highest point of the temple. 'If you are the Son of God,' he said, 'throw yourself down. For it is written: "He will command his angels concerning you, and they will lift you up in their hands, so that you will not strike your foot against a stone".' Jesus answered him, 'It is also written: "Do not put the Lord your God to the test".' Again, the devil took him to a very high mountain and showed him all the kingdoms of the world and their splendor. 'All this I will give you,' he said, 'if you will bow down and worship me.' Jesus said to him, 'Away from me, Satan! For it is written: "Worship the Lord your God, and serve him only".' Then the devil left him, and angels came and attended him."

Jesus was tempted with food, attention, power, and accomplishments. Had He surrendered to these temptations, He would have been given bread to comfort Him. He would have received incredible fame from those who witnessed His rescue by angels. He would have been given international power. And in the face of it all, Jesus chose the truth of God to overcome. Our prayer for this young generation is that the Holy Spirit would empower them, as they face loneliness, depression, and anxiety, to submit to God and to stand on His truth.

With this in mind, let's pray that the Holy Spirit's invitation to draw close to the Lord in their loneliness would be heard by the hearts of our young generation (Rev. 3:20). Pray that their eyes would be opened and their ears would hear His invitation to lean into God's ever-present love and leadership over their lives (Matt. 13:16-17).

Pray that they would be awakened to the need for in-person community around them. And if there are previous hurts or conflicts, there would be reconciliation between them and their brothers and sisters in Christ (Eph. 4:31-32). Pray that their connections with others would be fruitful in stirring greater hunger and growth in their walk with Christ (Heb. 10:24-25).

Pray that godly counselors and pastors would be able to help disciple and guide our young generation through healing and support to overcome years of loneliness, depression, and anxiety (Prov. 11:14,12:18). Pray for freedom to grow into their purpose and callings (1 John 5:4).

Pray that wisdom and truth would be on their lips as they step closer to the leadership that awaits them (Romans 12:6-8). As they become the next generation of pastors, missionaries, marketplace leaders, and especially mothers and fathers, may we pray that their impact and influence will further the generation after them into greater freedom and faith in Jesus Christ.

Find a supplementary worship-based prayer guide to this chapter in the respective appendix.

Please, also, join us in prayer for this day through the SR App or at strategicrenewal.com/21days

---

CHAPTER 10

DIGITAL DISCERNMENT AND SOCIAL MEDIA ENGAGEMENT

Justin Jeppesen

I VIVIDLY RECALL staring wide-eyed at the computer screen in my college resident director's office. It was 2007. And on the brick box of the laptop was a choppy promotional video of the launch of Apple's new iPhone. As I gazed at all the amazing features being touted, a twinge of covetousness arose within me. But I interrupted this temptation by blurting out, "I would never want one of those, it's just way too much!"

Fast forward 18 years and more than seven iPhones later, and I humbly need to eat my past words and confess that I have had, and still want to have, a smartphone. Yet more often than not, I continue to feel they are "way too much!" While research varies depending on the sources, a 2025 study suggests that people spend about 4 hours and 37 minutes per day on their phones. Astonishingly, that number jumps to 6 hours and 5 minutes for Gen Z, or those born roughly between 1997 and 2012. Furthermore, the average American checks their phone 205 times per day, which translates to picking up that glowing brick in their pocket once every seven minutes. Needless to say, the up-and-coming generations have been termed "digital natives" and "screen-agers" who have and are being formed in drastically different ways than older generations.

So, how does all of this pertain to how we can pray for the next generation? I believe the revelation of Philippians 4:8-9 provides a very helpful rubric and guide for how we can intercede.

Avoid Extremes

Rather than fully receiving or rejecting smartphones and social media, there are ways we can intentionally engage with them in a redemptive manner. Technology ought not to be idolized or demonized. Paul, writing from prison, gives the following admonition to the Philippian church:

"Finally, brothers, *whatever* is true, *whatever* is honorable, *whatever* is just, *whatever* is pure, *whatever* is lovely, *whatever* is commendable, if there is any excellence, if there is anything worthy of praise, think about these things" (Philippians 4:8).

The term "whatever" used here is repeated six times, which can encapsulate a broad range of topics. In our digital-saturated culture, it provides a redemptive roadmap for what we focus on and value most. We pray that the next generation will be guided by what is true, honorable, just, pure, lovely, and commendable in their use of smartphones and social media.

Curate Your Content

If we follow the course of Philippians 4:8, we will intentionally guard what comes into our minds. We can either curate our own content or have it curated for us. Rather than allowing an algorithm to dictate what we abide in, we can allow our adoration of truth and love to shape our thoughts, words, and actions. It's interesting, and even ironic, that social media platforms use discipleship-like language by gauging who we follow, which then determines what content we consume and create. Let's pray fervently that the next generation will not be discipled simply by scrolling on their newsfeed in isolation, but rather by searching and obeying the Scriptures in community.

Grace-filled Guardrails

I will be the first to admit that smartphone usage can be very addictive. Brain science will back up why this is the case and how our social media engagement has literally remapped our neurological pathways. While correlation is certainly not always causation, a plethora of research makes a compelling case that the spike in anxiety and depression is lock-step with the advent of and rise of the smartphone. This is why having healthy boundaries, or grace-filled guardrails on how much time we spend in the digital world, is so important and wise. Most young people readily acknowledge that their smartphone usage is a problem and are seeking practical alternatives to regulate and even detoxify from their digital habits.

May we pray for the next generation to establish intentional screen-time limits and even regular "digital fasting," so that they can prioritize in-person fellowship and eliminate distractions from what matters most. Pray for the wisdom of the Scriptures to cultivate godly discernment for digital engagement in all its various forms. Imagine if the next generation were to replace checking their phone 205 times a day with meditation on Scripture and seeking God's face in prayer!

Leverage Digital Platforms for Gospel Advancement

Rather than running the risk of scrolling our souls away, digital platforms have incredible potential for advancing God's Kingdom. Even though things like social media can oversaturate us with information and connectivity while depriving us of intimacy and actual connection, it does provide the opportunity for everyone to reach almost anyone in the world. The next generation is uniquely positioned to proclaim the gospel with grace and truth. Paul, the prison pastor, continues in Philippians 4:9 by boldly declaring, "What you have learned and received and heard and seen in me—*practice these things*, and the God of peace will be with you."

Pray that the next generation will leverage digital platforms as an extension of their discipleship, living deeply locally and sharing broadly globally. Pray that they would creatively reproduce what they have learned, received, heard, and seen from those who have faithfully modeled Christ. Pray for the Holy Spirit to give inspired and prophetic creativity to make content that draws people to the beauty and power of the gospel. Pray for unreached people groups around the world to be reached with testimonies of lives transformed by Christ and for them to encounter the good news of God's love, grace, and salvation.

Lastly, as the ever-changing landscape of the digital world continues to advance, may we pray for the Lord's redemptive power to be displayed in and through the next generation so that a gospel witness would resound to the uttermost parts of the earth.

Find a supplementary worship-based prayer guide to this chapter in the respective appendix.

Please, also, join us in prayer for this day through the SR App or at strategicrenewal.com/21days

---

CHAPTER 11

BUILDING A BIBLICAL WORLDVIEW

Len Crowley

Start from Scripture.

Honestly, it's as simple as that.

If we actually believe that God's Word is true, then there will be a corresponding outcome in how we "view the world." What *God says* in the Bible about the world, sin, evil, judgment, grace, salvation, and eternity will guide our thinking, reasoning, relationships, words, and activities. Hence, our "worldview" emerges through believing and trusting in what He says in His Word. If *our lives are truly grounded in Scripture—and we submit* to its teachings—we will align our lives, thoughts, and behaviors with reality and honor God.

What more is there? How better to demonstrate our reliance upon the Lord Jesus and His work, both at the Cross and daily in the transforming of our hearts and controlling of the cultures in which we live? This is the foundation of a biblical worldview, and one that will more than stand the test of time and circumstance.

"What does the Text say?" is our first question when we face curious, troubling, or even "normal" circumstances in our world. And aligning our thoughts and behavior to what the Lord does say in His Word—not what we sometimes have been told that it says—will lead us along a level path.

So, we begin with "The Book." Our familiarity with the Bible and what it tells us is paramount. How are we, then, burying the treasure of Scripture deep into our lives? Are we reading, meditating, thinking, and resting in that supernatural resource? Are our lives reflective of trust in Him and the way things "really are?" Are we seeing Holy Spirit-inspired transformation, changes in both the way we think and behave? A quick—and necessarily honest—self-assessment will reveal whether we *really do* follow God's Word or "man's," for they are fundamentally different.

Harry Blamires, the British author of *A Christian Mind*, writing in the 1950's (though he may just as well have been writing yesterday), concludes summarily: "The secular mind and the truly Christian mind are in violent conflict." There is no middle ground.

So, the questions I must ask myself are: What informs my thinking, my life choices, my words, and my reactions? Do I know—and truly trust—Scripture? Do I know what it says about certain popular and current issues? Do I obey what I know to do? Do I repent when I do not? All of this is consistent with seeking to walk in this world by God's leading, not our own.

For example, ask yourself, "What does the Bible say about obedience? About honoring God? About worship? About our deceitful and 'desperately wicked,' rebellious hearts?" Importantly, can we see the character and quality of His life developing in us? If you belong to Him, that will become increasingly evident. And it will not, if you do not.

What does it say about prayer? How deeply is biblical prayer a part of our daily lives? Jesus emphasized the importance and vitality of corporate prayer, particularly in Matthew 6:9-13. That

4-part model prayer should guide us as we pray together, because that's how He commanded us to pray. Prayer like that proves that the genuine intent of our lives in this realm is to live dependent on God and His power, not our own.

Following obediently in prayer, loving God in heart and in mind, soul, and strength, will prove out by how we view and respond to circumstances—both tragic and delightful. Are we overwhelmed? Are we stable despite the rocky circumstances and difficult, sad portions of our journey in this life? Our reactions amid turmoil or joy, in "plenty and want," go a long way in proving that we really do trust what God says in His Word.

In short, then, if we truly trust what Scripture says—and what the Holy Spirit confirms in His multifaceted ways—we will think and behave in an "other-worldly" way. Our thoughts will be guided by heaven and God's agenda (Col. 3:1-4). We will not fear the adversary nor his wiles and temptations, nor his minions and their attacks. And we will present to both the Lord and the world a heart of wisdom, a life of contentment, a passion for Him, and enormous grace for one another.

As to our worldview, that's the "proof in the pudding." So may we pray these truths into the lives of the next generation. Pray for the Lord of heaven and earth to give them hearts that start with Scripture, minds brimming with the Text, so that their live's embody what the Book says.

Find a supplementary worship-based prayer guide to this chapter in the respective appendix.

Please, also, join us in prayer for this day through the SR App or at strategicrenewal.com/21days

CHAPTER 12

RESISTING CULTURAL CONFORMITY

Amber Doggett

> *"And do not be conformed to this world, but be transformed by the renewing of your mind, that you may prove what is that good and acceptable and perfect will of God" (Romans 12:2).*

Have you ever felt insecure, like you didn't fit in? What makes us want (mostly unknowingly) to conform to the world? We all long for acceptance, pursue what brings us pleasure, and are constantly trying to find our purpose. Conforming to the world puts us on a perpetual hamster wheel of fake performance and trying to gain all three of these things, without an end in sight! Whatever we think we are, or are trying to be, we will never measure up.

Paul lays out the solution pretty clearly: "Be transformed by the renewing of your mind."

Renewing our minds is a daily surrender to God's will. Jesus gives us purpose. Jesus calls us to be the supporting character of our story, and He asks to be the lead. When we commit to a daily surrender to Jesus, laying down our desires and wants to Him, our identities are in Him. We are saying out loud, "Lord, Your will is better than mine. Amen!" We then trust and obey, and are faithful in whatever that particular day brings us, all for His glory. This is true freedom—this is living life abundantly.

True renewal of the mind should include being surrendered daily to reading God's Word. The Word of God is how we get to know our amazing Creator. Hebrews 4:12 says, "For the word of God is living and active, sharper than any two-edged sword, piercing to the division of soul and of spirit, of joints and of marrow, and discerning the thoughts and intentions of the heart." May we never be too busy to be in God's Word. It is a gift from our Savior; may we never take it for granted. Read the Bible daily and write God's Word on your heart through Scripture memorization. These things will bring life and renew your mind.

Renewal of the mind also includes daily conversation with Jesus through prayer. Colossians 4:2 says, "Continue steadfastly in prayer, being watchful in it with thanksgiving." Praise Jesus through prayer, worship Him, and praise His name! May we never get over the awe and wonder of who our Creator is, and how wonderful He is, and how worthy His name is. Pray for His will, and pray for a daily renewal of your mind. If we aren't praying and reading God's Word, do we even have a relationship with Jesus at all? It's an important question to ask ourselves daily. May Jesus always be given our best and daily worship and surrender.

The renewing of the mind also includes the environments we put ourselves in. Who do you surround yourself with? What are you watching online or on television? What books are you reading, and do they bring life or death to you? My husband and I are parenting preteen twins. We have had many conversations with them about friendships, and how who they hang out with is who they will likely start to act like or even become. This is the same for us as adults. It reminds me of the song "Oh, be careful little ears what you hear! Oh, be careful little eyes what you see!" (Are you singing it with me, too?)

Jesus has called us to live in community with each other. May we be praying for godly people who will point us to Jesus and love us enough to be honest with us in this life. Godly friendships and community are a gift from God. We are all human; we will sin and mess up. However, when we seek godly counsel and wisdom from those who point us back to Jesus in all circumstances, we have found true friendship and true family.

Conforming to this world is easy, but those who take the narrow path will find life. They will find true freedom that only Jesus can offer. Pray, seek God's face, read His Word, and seek wise counsel every single day. Surround yourself with godly people who will lead you to Jesus in everything that comes your way. This is the way to renew your mind, and it's a daily surrender. Jesus is the only one who can provide a full life, lived abundantly. He longs to give us such a life; we just have to be brave enough and wise enough to reach for it. The next time you are tempted to respond the way the world does to life, remember, if you are a follower of Jesus, you are His! Do not turn inward, do not turn to the world for answers—turn to Jesus.

Isaiah 43:1 says, "Fear not, for I have redeemed you; I have called you by name, you are mine." We're His! We belong to the King of Kings, the Lord of Lords. We are His children. Let Him take the lead in your story as pray these truths into our lives and the lives of the next generation—you won't regret it!

Find a supplementary worship-based prayer guide to this chapter in the respective appendix.

Please, also, join us in prayer for this day through the SR App or at strategicrenewal.com/21days

---

CHAPTER 13

COURAGEOUS FAITH IN CRISIS AND SUFFERING

Katie Laitkep

> *"In this you rejoice, though now for a little while, if necessary, you have been grieved by various trials, so that the tested genuineness of your faith—more precious than gold that perishes though it is tested by fire—may be found to result in praise and glory and honor at the revelation of Jesus Christ" (1 Peter 1:6–7).*

What is the earliest moment you remember? When you think back to your first few years of life, can you picture the face of a family member smiling down on you, the way the sky looked from your stroller, or the bright lights of a particular room? Maybe it was a darker moment that imprinted itself on your heart and mind from an early age, a jarring image or sound that shook your memory awake.

I remember being three years old, pulling on blue gloves and a gown, and visiting my newborn twin brothers, who were wrapped in wires in the NICU. It wasn't until decades later, when I began undergoing medical treatment as a teenager and then began working as a hospital teacher in a pediatric unit, that I realized how suffering had framed my whole life.

We think we can protect younger generations from painful moments. We try to keep childhood unmarked by sorrow, but the reality is that by the time young people reach adulthood, many are carrying the weight of family conflict, the implications of diagnoses, the uncertainty of global crises they don't understand, and other difficult situations.

The next generation's faith is being forged in real time, as they encounter sin and suffering from their own front-row seat. They face the temptation to rewrite their beliefs about God based on how they view any given situation. They see bad things happen and assume that God can't be good. When life feels unfair, they assume God must be as well. They explicitly ask the same questions many of us do in the midst of suffering: *Why is this happening? Where is God? If He allows all of this to happen, can I really trust Him?*

The answers to those questions matter, and when the younger generation sees the truth of who God is—when they experience His faithfulness, His presence, and His promises—it lays a foundation they're able to fall back on the rest of their lives. Their glimpses of God, knowing He's with them in the fire, helps to ground them in hope, shape their character, and grow faith that will remain when future crises come.

Faith Forged in the Fire

When suffering enters our lives, it's often a painful surprise, but Jesus told His followers to expect it: "In the world you *will* have tribulation," he said (John 16:33, emphasis added). At the same time, He didn't leave them without hope. As He told the disciples, "I have said these things to you, so that in me you may have peace... take heart; I have overcome the world" (v. 33).

This verse helps answer some of the most profound questions that impact our faith during a crisis. *Why does suffering happen?* As believers, we are *in Christ*, but we also still live "in the world" (v. 33). We live in a world system with a real enemy who opposes the message of Jesus, and this side of heaven, we'll continue to encounter the effects of sin and suffering.

Where is God? He is in the same place that He was when His own Son bore the weight of the world on the cross. He could have left us without a solution to the grief, pain, and crises of our day, but in His sovereignty and kindness, He sent Jesus, who has "overcome the world." The victory we experience now in part, we'll one day know in full.

If He allows all of this to happen, can I really trust Him? Where else would we go? Jesus promises, "In me you may have peace." The Lord is not distant or silent; Jesus has gone before us in suffering so that He may walk with us. Our trust isn't anchored in the absence of pain, but in Christ alone, who is making all things new.

This perspective is why the Apostle Peter was able to weave joy into his teachings on suffering. In 1 Peter 1:6-7, he reminds believers that trials, while painful, are not meaningless. His encouragement provides a framework for us to pray for the next generation as they face various trials.

Pray for them to:

- Rejoice in the living hope they have in Christ, which is theirs in all circumstances (v. 6).

- Remember trials are temporary and that eternity is nearer than they think (v. 6).

- Be quick to bring their grief to God and to experience His comfort for every hurt (v. 6).
- Own their faith personally and authentically, not merely claiming the beliefs of their parents or peers (v. 7).
- Cling to Christ when their faith is tested, responding with obedience and hope (v. 7).
- See the value of tested faith as more precious than anything the world offers (v. 7).
- Accept suffering as part of God's refining work, which produces perseverance, courage, and Christlike character (v. 7).
- Reflect Jesus in the midst of their pain, allowing their tested faith to result in praise, glory, and honor to His name (v. 7).

It's often through crises and suffering that a young believer moves from knowing *about* Jesus to knowing Him personally. In painful moments, they come to see that while having His gifts is good—gifts like health, comfort, and security—having Him is far, far greater.

May this be a generation whose faith in suffering proves that Jesus is near and that He is enough. As they walk through various trials in the days ahead, may they be found standing with what cannot be destroyed: genuine, courageous faith in Jesus, of greater worth than gold.

Find a supplementary worship-based prayer guide to this chapter in the respective appendix.

Please, also, join us in prayer for this day through the SR App or at strategicrenewal.com/21days

CHAPTER 14

SPIRIT-FILLED LIVING

Daniel Henderson

EVERY GENERATION HAS FACED its unique challenges and opportunities. Yet, in God's providence, there seems to be an unmistakable urgency surrounding the spiritual formation of Gen Z. This generation is marked by remarkable creativity, technological fluency, and social awareness. But it is also plagued by unprecedented anxiety, identity confusion, and cultural disorientation. If there were ever a generation that needed to know—not just intellectually, but experientially—what it means to live under the control and power of the indwelling Holy Spirit, it is this one.

The Biblical Foundation

Jesus made it clear to His disciples that the Christian life is impossible apart from the Spirit's empowering presence. He told them, "It is to your advantage that I go away...for if I do not go away, the Helper will not come to you" (John 16:7). The promise of the Spirit was not a theological accessory but the essential provision for living faithfully and fruitfully in a fallen world.

The Apostle Paul reinforced this when he wrote, "Do not get drunk with wine...but be filled with the Spirit" (Eph. 5:18). The Spirit-filled life is not optional—it is the very essence of Christian living. Without Him, we cannot walk in holiness, bear witness with boldness, or manifest the love of Christ in our relationships.

If this is true for all believers, then how much more urgent is it that we help Gen Z, who are bombarded daily with distractions and distortions, to experience and embrace the Spirit's control and power?

The Cultural Climate

Sociologists tell us that Gen Z is the most anxious, lonely, and digitally distracted generation in history. They live in a constant stream of information, but often lack the wisdom to filter truth from lies. They are deeply connected online, but often feel profoundly disconnected in real life. They care about justice and authenticity, but struggle to anchor those values in transcendent truth.

Only the Spirit of God can meet these deep longings. He is the Comforter for their anxiety, the Counselor for their confusion, and the Source of authentic community in the body of Christ. He provides clarity in a world of chaos and boldness in a culture of compromise.

No clever program, no flashy platform, no eloquent sermon will ultimately satisfy the hunger of their souls. They need the transforming presence of Christ made real through the indwelling Spirit.

The Practical Implications

So how do we help Gen Z grasp and live out this reality?

1. **Teach them the truth of the Spirit's indwelling.**
   Many young believers know about the Holy Spirit in vague terms, but few understand that He is a Person who permanently dwells within them from the moment of salvation.

They must learn that the Spirit is not some impersonal force that is summoned from a distant location through the enthusiasm of their singing but the very presence of God, mediated only by the finished work of Christ and equipping them to know Him and make Him known.

2. **Model a Spirit-filled life.**
   Teaching without example is empty. If we, as parents, pastors, and leaders, are not living in daily surrender to the Spirit, our words will ring hollow. Gen Z longs for authenticity. They can spot hypocrisy instantly. What will grip them most is not a lecture about the Spirit but a life empowered by Him.

3. **Guide them into Spirit-led prayer.**
   Prayer is where the theology of the Spirit becomes experiential reality. When young people learn to pray Scripture-fed, Spirit-led, worship-based prayers, they move beyond self-centered petitions to genuine communion with God. This is where the Spirit teaches, convicts, comforts, and empowers in ways no classroom can replicate.

4. **Equip them for mission.**
   Gen Z has a passion for purpose. They want to make a difference in the world. We must show them that the Spirit does not indwell them simply for personal comfort, but for global impact. The Holy Spirit is a witness-bearing Spirit. Acts 1:8 reminds us that the Spirit comes to empower us to boldly tell of a risen Savior. When Gen Z experiences the

Spirit's power in mission, they will taste the joy of partnering with God in His redemptive plan.

The Urgency of Now

We cannot afford to delay. Studies reveal that a majority of Gen Z are leaving the church by the time they reach young adulthood. If we do not ground them in the reality of the Spirit-filled life now, they will be swept away by the tides of secularism, cynicism, and despair.

But there is also reason for great hope. Throughout history, revival has often begun with the young. Think of the students at Haystack, the young preachers of the Great Awakening, or the college revivals that have sparked movements of prayer and mission. Could it be that if Gen Z discovers the reality of the Spirit's indwelling presence, they could lead the way into the next great renewal?

Our Call as Leaders

Strategic Renewal exists to call the church back to the priority of Scripture-fed, Spirit-led, worship-based prayer. But this vision cannot be limited to pastors or seasoned saints. It must be passed to the next generation. We must invest intentionally in Gen Z, praying for them, mentoring them, and giving them opportunities to experience the Spirit's transforming work.

The Apostle John wrote, "I have no greater joy than to hear that my children are walking in the truth" (3 John 4). What greater joy could we know than to see a generation rise up—controlled by the Spirit, empowered for mission, walking in holiness, and marked by authentic worship?

Conclusion

The future of the church is not in better strategies, more compelling personalities, or larger platforms. It is in the biblical demonstration of the Spirit-filled life to the next generation. Gen Z does not need to be entertained; they need to be empowered. They do not need to be coddled; they need to be called into the Spirit's control. They do not need to be impressed by us; they need to be indwelt by Him.

Our task is clear. We must pray, teach, model, and equip. And we must do it with urgency, humility, and faith. For if Gen Z learns to walk in the Spirit's power, we may well witness the renewal for which we have long prayed.

Find a supplementary worship-based prayer guide to this chapter in the respective appendix.

Please, also, join us in prayer for this day through the SR App or at strategicrenewal.com/21days

---

CHAPTER 15

MARKS OF A TRUE MOVE OF GOD—SPIRITUAL OPENNESS AND THE GOSPEL

Justin Jeppesen

> *"Let love be genuine. Abhor what is evil; hold fast to what is good. Love one another with brotherly affection. Outdo one another in showing honor" (Romans 12:9-10).*

God is moving powerfully in the next generation. Studies show younger generations are the most spiritually open, and we're seeing the proof of it in the droves of college students filling campus squares, beaches, chapels, and stadiums seeking a genuine encounter with the living God. Yet, despite all of this, many remain skeptical—and often rightly so.

How can we, as Christians, rightly discern a true move of God? That question has echoed across centuries of church history. Each generation faces moments of renewal and revival, and with them, the challenge of discerning the genuine from the artificial. Thankfully, Scripture provides us with a trustworthy rubric.

Romans 12 marks a turning point in Paul's letter. Following the rich theological truths of the first eleven chapters, Paul pivots to application to reveal what the gospel looks like embodied in

God's people. In Romans 12:9–21, we're ushered into a blueprint for Christian community—a portrait of who God wants us to be and what He desires us to do, especially as we pray for the next generation.

Paul opens with this powerful exhortation: *"Let love be genuine."* Literally, "Let love be without hypocrisy." Here is the dividing line between what is real and what is fake. The word Paul uses refers to a love that is sincere, supernatural, and self-giving, without pretense or performance.

The litmus test of genuine Christianity, and every true move of God, is love.

A true move of God will always turn His people from counterfeit love toward genuine love.

The Right Ingredients

At first glance, Romans 12:9–21 can feel like a rapid-fire list of commands, almost a "ragbag" of unrelated instructions. Yet each imperative adds a fresh ingredient to Paul's recipe for genuine love.

I've come to appreciate this through my recent hobby of baking bread. When I was learning to bake, I made all sorts of mistakes—forgetting the leaven, leaving out the oil, or skipping the salt. Each ingredient seemed small, but without them, the loaf never turned out right.

In the same way, Paul lists several "ingredients" of love, many of which are "one another" statements found throughout the New Testament. These commands function like spiritual arteries that carry the life of Christ through His body. And among them, three stand out as key ingredients:

1. Love one another with familial affection.

2. Outdo one another in showing honor.

3. Live in harmony with one another.

Each one moves us deeper into the heart of genuine love, and together, they form the character of a true move of God and a pathway of praying for a genuine move of God in the next generation.

1. **A True Move of God Restores the Church to Love One Another with Familial Affection**

   Here we move from distance to devoted discernment. Like leaven in bread, this ingredient causes all the others to rise. Without it, everything falls flat.

   It might seem strange that the command to love genuinely is followed by a command to hate —*"Abhor what is evil; cling to what is good."* But true love is discerning. It's not blind sentimentality or emotional indulgence. It's a love so devoted to the beloved that it hates whatever threatens their flourishing. Genuine love refuses to tolerate what destroys.

   We live in a time when distance has dulled our discernment. The past several years of pandemic, polarization, and digital detachment have left many of us distant from one another. We've criticized, assumed, or ignored each other, rather than loving each other with family-like affection. But you cannot discern from a distance. Love requires proximity, especially with those who differ from us.

Jesus declared that the world would know we are His disciples by our love for one another (John 13:34-35). When the next generation sees this kind of love—not political allegiance, not polished programs, but family-like affection—they will know the gospel is real.

2. **A True Move of God Restores Honor in Our Relationships**

   Next, we move from validating our opinions to valuing others above ourselves.

   This ingredient is like oil in the bread; it binds everything together into a cohesive whole.

   The word *honor* literally means "to assign value." In our culture, we assign value by price tags and status, but in God's economy, value is defined by creation and redemption. Every person is made in God's image and purchased by the blood of Christ. That's the ultimate price tag of worth.

   So how do we "outdo one another" in showing honor, as Paul commands? He gives us a few ways to pray into:

   - **By generosity**: "Contribute to the needs of the saints" (Romans 12:13). Love shares life and possessions so that none are left in need.
   - **By hospitality**: "Seek to show hospitality." Generosity cares for those we know; hospitality welcomes those we don't. It makes space for strangers, and even enemies, to become friends and family.

- **By sympathy**: "Rejoice with those who rejoice, weep with those who weep." Love doesn't stay aloof. It draws near. It suffers and sings in solidarity.

When a generation sees a church that honors rather than devalues, that welcomes rather than excludes, that celebrates others' victories rather than envies them, then they begin to see Jesus. So may we pray for a renewal of honor among the generations within the Church!

3. **A True Move of God Restores Relational Harmony**

We move from haughtiness to humility.

This ingredient is like the salt in bread; it's subtle, yet vital. It preserves freshness and brings flavor. Without humility, love grows stale.

Paul writes, *"Live in harmony with one another. Do not be haughty, but associate with the lowly."* Harmony and humility are inseparable. To be humble is to know your place in relation to others and to rejoice in your part in God's divine symphony.

The problem is that we often compare our voices to those of others. We treat the body of Christ like a competition rather than a collaboration. We want to sing lead when only Jesus can carry the melody. The Spirit calls us instead to harmonize, to align our lives with the melody of the gospel.

In a world filled with noise, outrage, and division, spiritual openness begins with humility. It's the openness to listen to God and to one another. Romans 12:16 literally reads, "Think the same thing toward one another." May we pray diligently for the next generation to experience harmony in the Church and to find their voice within the body so that the Church will further become a "house of prayer for the nations" (Mark 11:17).

Participating in a True Move of God

A true move of God, then, is marked not by hype, but by holiness; not by emotion alone, but by transformation; not by crowds, but by compassion. It is repentance from our failure to love and a return to our first love, Jesus.

Beloved, the Christian life is not a hard life to live; it's an impossible one. These marks cannot be produced by human effort. They are born of the enabling grace of the indwelling Spirit of Christ.

What is impossible with man is always possible with God!

So as we long for a move of God in our day, especially for the next generation, may we seek not just the manifestations of revival, but the marks of love. May we depend on God's grace to live Romans 12, becoming a people whose genuine love points the world to a genuine Savior.

When love is real, the gospel becomes irresistible. When love is genuine, the next generation sees Jesus.

And that, dear friends, is the truest mark of a move of God.

Find a supplementary worship-based prayer guide to this chapter in the respective appendix.

Please, also, join us in prayer for this day through the SR App or at strategicrenewal.com/21days

---

CHAPTER 16

GOSPEL BOLDNESS AND WITNESS

Paul Worcester

Read Acts 4

The need of the hour for reaching this next generation is not new methods for evangelism but new boldness! Every genuine revival has been marked by bold and broad gospel sowing. As the National Collegiate Director for the North American Mission Board, I have a front-row seat to what God is doing on campuses. The churches and ministries that see the most students come to Christ are those unashamed to proclaim the exclusivity of the gospel and who equip every student to join the front lines of reaching their peers. The best person to reach a student with the gospel is another student!

In Acts 4, Peter boldly declared Jesus as the only way to salvation, even reminding the council that they had killed Him! "Salvation is found in no one else, for there is no other name under heaven given to mankind by which we must be saved" (Acts 4:12).

This generation is flocking to ministries that unflinchingly roar the gospel and teach the hard truths about God's holiness, sin, hell, and Jesus as the only substitute and narrow way to eternal life. As I preach to thousands of college students each year, the messages that hit hardest are the old-school ones about the urgency of eternity and the exclusivity of Christ. It's a myth that students don't care about eternal realities. I regularly see students huddled in prayer, weeping over the lostness of friends and family. As revival is stirring, the Spirit is producing a supernatural burden for the lost that fuels a boldness God is using in almost unbelievable ways. We're not just seeing individuals saved, we are seeing whole friend groups come to Christ at the same time!

My wife Christy discipled a college student named Larissa last year through our Good Soil Discipleship School on the North Shore of Oahu. Part of her training included weekly evangelism at the University of Hawaii and daily prayer for B.O.B. (Burden for the lost, Opportunity to witness, and Boldness to share Christ). When Larissa returned to Kennesaw State, God gave her a deep burden for her campus. She gathered a few friends for weekly evangelism and prayer walking, crying out for God to move. In time, they felt led to host a united night of student-led worship and gospel preaching at the outdoor amphitheater in the center of campus. Word spread organically, and hundreds of students showed up! That night, one bold student preached a raw, unfiltered gospel, calling classmates to repent and trust Christ. Many came forward to surrender their lives to Jesus, while others confessed sin and were prayed over. What started with one student's burden sparked a campus-wide move of God. When I think of these students, I'm reminded of Acts 4:13, "Now when they saw the boldness of Peter and John, and perceived that they were uneducated, common men, they were astonished. And they recognized that they had been with Jesus."

The problem is not with the harvest. The harvest is plentiful. The problem is a lack of laborers (Matt. 9:36-38). That means there are many young people right now who would come to Christ if a laborer loved them, prayed for them, and shared the gospel with them. This is the greatest tragedy I can imagine, that there are more young people willing to hear and respond to the gospel than there are Christians willing to share Christ with them!

Years ago, when I was starting a new college ministry at California State University, Chico, I remember driving to campus to evangelize while battling discouragement. Thoughts ran through my head like, *"You're just bothering students"* or *"If you share too soon, you'll push them away."* In that moment of spiritual warfare, a verse I had memorized flashed into my mind: "And the Lord said to Paul one night in a vision, 'Do not be afraid, but go on speaking and do not be silent, for I am with you, and no one will attack you to harm you, for I have many in this city who are my people' " (Acts 18:9–10). It was as if the Holy Spirit whispered, *"I have many people on this campus. I'm already working in students' hearts and it's your job to go find them."* In that moment, I had a surge of faith and joy when I realized God had already gone before me, preparing students to respond to the gospel. God is already sovereignly at work among young people. We just get the joy of discovering the ripe ones. I call it the divine Easter egg hunt. Our job is to love, pray, and share; God's job is to draw, convict, and convert.

A few years later, God had blessed our disciple-making efforts with fifty hungry student leaders eager to reach our campus. At our back-to-school retreat, I threw out a challenge, *"What would happen if we shared the gospel with 1,000 students this school year?"* From the back, one of the skater bros shot up his hand and sarcastically said, *"I think some people would get saved!"* After we all laughed, the simplicity of that truth hit us. We may not have been the brightest at Chico State, but at least we understood that there is a direct connection to how many people you share the gospel with and how many you lead to Christ! After some quick math, we realized that if each of us had just one gospel conversation a week, we could share with 1,000 students. We broke into small groups and turned to Acts 4:29–31, using it as a guide for our prayers. God met us powerfully at that retreat, launching us into the most fruitful year of ministry we had ever experienced. By year's end, we only hit 600 conversations, but 207 students made decisions to follow Jesus! Almost every day, our private group thread blew up with updates of our students leading their peers to Christ.

A recent study by Barna showed that "two-thirds of Gen Z are highly or moderately spiritually open."[1] Young people are as open as ever to hearing and responding to the gospel if they're approached in a sincere and personal way. What they long for isn't flashy lights and fancy programs; it's genuine love and personal discipleship.

We're seeing a nationwide movement of low-pressure, intentional evangelism through what I call "gospel appointments," which is simply a set time to share the gospel.[2] Our goal is to set up a gospel appointment with every student who visits our church or ministry events. Student leaders and staff mingle with new students, inviting them to lunch or coffee to get to know them and

---

[1] https://www.barna.com/research/spiritual-openness/

[2] https://www.gensend.org/resource/how-to-share-jesus-using-gospel-appointments/

share more about the group, because after all, we are all about the gospel!

My closing challenge to you is to start setting up gospel appointments with students you meet. What could happen if pastors and leaders aimed for one a week and brought along students they were training? Millions of young people are just one conversation away from giving their lives to Christ. As you model this lifestyle, students will catch the vision, and you may just spark a movement!

Use Acts 4 as a guide for your prayers. Pray for young people in your life and on campuses and universities in your area, that God will give believing students the boldness to share their faith. Start praying B.O.B. for yourself daily (Burden, Opportunities, Boldness).

Find a supplementary worship-based prayer guide to this chapter in the respective appendix.

Please, also, join us in prayer for this day through the SR App or at strategicrenewal.com/21days

---

CHAPTER 17

GLOBAL VISION AND MISSIONAL HEART

Katie Laitkep

> *"You will be my witnesses in Jerusalem and in all Judea and Samaria, and to the end of the earth"* (Acts 1:8).

If you've been to a kindergarten graduation, you've seen the chaos that comes when five- and six-year-olds are lined up in a room filled with their family members. In recent years, as teachers have announced what the kids hope to be when they "grow up," their answers have increasingly included nods to the digital age: they want to be stars on any number of social media platforms, professional gamers, influencers, or viral creators with the success they've seen modeled. Even at a young age, the craving for visibility, applause, and recognition appeals to them.

It's not a new desire. In the Gospels, as Jesus' fame spread, the young disciples wrestled with their own longings for recognition, status, and honor. In Mark 10:35–37, James and John approached Jesus and said to Him, "Grant us to sit, one at your right hand and one at your left, in your glory." But Jesus, as He led the way to the cross, was about to teach them about a radically different kind of greatness, one found not in making a name for themselves, but in pointing the whole world to His.

Living Testimonies of the Gospel

At the conclusion of Jesus' bodily ministry on earth, He left His disciples with a final message: "But you will receive power when the Holy Spirit has come upon you, and you will be my witnesses in Jerusalem and in all Judea and Samaria, and to the end of the earth" (Acts 1:8). This imperative not only shaped their future calling, but today, it provides us a framework to pray for the next generation, who the Lord is raising up to bring His light to the ends of the earth.

> "*You* will be my witnesses."

Jesus could have chosen the most politically connected, the richest, or the most educated men to be part of His plan to rescue the world. Instead, He called a group of ordinary fishermen, who were young and impulsive and still had much to learn, even after years of walking beside Him.

Jesus saw beyond their inexperience and missteps. Through the empowerment of the Holy Spirit, the disciples were able to articulate the gospel with boldness and clarity they'd never had before (Acts 1:8).

The same Spirit who empowered the disciples to "go into all the world and proclaim the gospel to the whole creation" (Mark 16:15) is alive in young believers today, including those who feel unqualified and unequipped to play a meaningful part in God's mission.

- Pray the next generation will receive the message of the gospel with deep conviction (1 Thess. 1:5).

- Pray they will be so moved by the reality of Jesus that they speak to others with the confidence of one who knows Him personally (Acts 4:13).
- Pray they will depend fully on the Lord, not operating by their own might or strength, but by the Spirit (Zech. 4:6).

"You will be *my witnesses.*"

Jesus didn't commission His disciples to promote themselves, to advance their own kingdom, or to chase a platform. They weren't called to be celebrities, but saints—dying to themselves, taking up their crosses daily, and following the example of their Savior, who had humbled himself to the point of death (Luke 9:23; Phil. 2:7–8).

Believers today have also been called to be heralds of the good news, telling the world: "There is no distinction between Jew and Greek; for the same Lord is Lord of all, bestowing his riches on all who call on him. For 'everyone who calls on the name of the Lord will be saved' " (Rom. 10:12–13).

- Pray that the next generation will die to themselves and understand that their words, actions, and daily lives are meant to point others to Him (Rom. 10:15).
- Pray they won't be ashamed of the testimony about our Lord but will speak the truth without fear (2 Tim. 1:7–8).
- Pray they live with eternal perspective, so their lives testify to the power of the gospel (2 Cor. 4:16–18).

"You will be my witnesses *in Jerusalem and in all Judea and Samaria, and to the end of the earth.*"

When Jesus gave His Great Commission, He told His followers to make disciples not just among their neighbors but "of all nations" (Matt. 28:19). We know that one day, "all tribes and peoples and languages" will stand before the throne and before the Lamb" (Rev. 7:9).

The question is: how will people from every nation join heaven's worship if they do not know Jesus? "How are they to believe in him of whom they have never heard?" (Rom. 10:14) Even now, the Lord is raising up members of the next generation who realize the eternal stakes that hang in the balance and who are willing to risk their lives so all may know Him.

1. Pray the next generation will see the lost as Jesus sees them, cultivating compassion that drives action (Luke 19:10).

2. Pray the Lord will raise up and send out countless young men and women to carry His gospel to those who have never heard His name (Matt. 9:37–38).

3. Pray for them to embrace the privilege of participating in God's redemptive plan, eager to see God glorified across the globe (Psalm 96:3).

A Generation on Mission

When you look at the next generation, as you observe a group still growing in their maturity and faith, you may not think of these young people as world-changers—yet they are part of God's Plan A to reach all of creation with the love of Christ.

Pray fervently for these young disciples. What may seem like youth and inexperience in human eyes can certainly become, in God's hands, a force for the kingdom: a generation that carries the gospel forth, witnessing to the truth and grace of Jesus with darkness-shaking boldness that will impact lives for eternity.

Find a supplementary worship-based prayer guide to this chapter in the respective appendix.

Please, also, join us in prayer for this day through the SR App or at strategicrenewal.com/21days

---

CHAPTER 18

REVIVAL AND AWAKENING

Len Crowley

"Find where God is working and join Him."

That was the central theme and focus given by Henry Blackaby a generation ago in his seminal work *Experiencing God.* It still applies.

Revival and awakening are works of God—not humans, regardless of how earnestly we pray for them. Despite our great desire and even our passionate prayers to see the Lord "move" in this generation, this is the place of true dependence and reliance. "Please," our hearts cry to the Father. Oh God, only You can do it! It echoes Peter's assertion in John 6:68, "Lord, to whom shall we go? You (alone) have the **words** of **eternal life**."

Such a plea is in sync with what the Lord Jesus taught us. He said very clearly in Matthew 16:18, "... *I will build* My Church, and the gates of Hell shall not prevail against it." HE will build. He will do the work—and He invites us to join Him. That was Blackaby's message.

But let us be clear: the works of justification, salvation, sanctification, transformation, reviving "lukewarm" believers, and awakening "ice cold" non-believers have always been initiated by God, not by our passion, preaching, or arguing. It begins and ends with God

Himself. "Not a result of works (our works, even good works—like prayer), so that no one may boast" (Eph. 2:8-10).

Nevertheless, the Lord Jesus does invite us into *His work* through our participation in prayer. Though this is a great mystery, for He even initiates that. Our longing for Christian revival and worldwide awakening (which are distinct) is initiated by His Spirit within us (Rom. 8:25-27).

For the Christian, to be *revived* is to return to or be re-energized for the things we did when we first trusted Christ (Rev. 2:4-5). Remember your initial enthrall, your "early believer enthusiasm?" It is of vital importance for each of us to look in the mirror daily and ask, am I loving Christ with the passion of His Spirit in me? Am I becoming "lukewarm?" Have I drifted into neglect in prayer, in obedience, in believing He WILL act? If so, Blackaby's invitation is spot on. "Find where God is working and join Him." In this, you will be "revived."

For the non-believer's condition, a better word is "awakening." Really, those without Christ are dead (spiritually). There is no life in them at present (Eph. 2:1-6). "You must be born again" is the message Jesus gave to Nicodemus in John 3:3 (who happened to be a "Teacher of Israel," v. 9). However, he didn't understand it—instead, he misunderstood.

To be fair, the words Jesus uses, *"gennaetha anothen" in Greek, mean "born from above" or "born anew,"* although they have been translated often as "born again." What Jesus was telling Nicodemus was that he was *not* alive. And there was no mystical "second blessing" or "second birth." Jesus was saying, "You are dead, Nicodemus. You need to be made alive *for the first time!"* In this, Jesus was alluding to Genesis 2:7, where Adam is "made alive" with the life of God as He breathed into him.

In both cases—*revival* from Christian apathy that needs a "re-ignition," or *awakening* that brings a non-believer to true eternal life—God is the origin, initiator, and sustainer. And so, and still, we pray. Lord, do Your work among us and the next generation today. Bring revival to Your church and salvation to those You call to Yourself for the first time in this hour. Let those who call on the name of the Lord see and experience Your great work within them and then in their cultures as You, once again, bring "light" to the world through their lives and the evident changes You are creating in them (Phil. 1:6).

Pray, then, because the Lord invites us to "enter His labor" with Him to see rejuvenation take place among those who already name the Name of Christ, and on behalf of those who don't love Jesus...yet!

> *And he said to them, "The harvest is plentiful, but the laborers are few. Therefore, pray earnestly to the Lord of the harvest to send out laborers into his harvest."*
>
> Luke 10:2 (cf. Matt. 9:38)

Find a supplementary worship-based prayer guide to this chapter in the respective appendix.

Please, also, join us in prayer for this day through the SR App or at strategicrenewal.com/21days

---

CHAPTER 19

MULTIPLICATION OF DISCIPLE-MAKERS

Paul Worcester

Read 2 Timothy 2:1-10

All my life, I have been haunted by my multiplication tables. As a kid, my mom spent hours quizzing me with those stupid flash cards! Now I'm haunted by multiplication in a different way. I am overwhelmed by the exponential power of personal disciple-making. It's the difference between addition and multiplication.

In this chapter, I want to do more than encourage you to pray for the next generation—I want to challenge you to *invest* in them. You may preach to hundreds each week, but your greatest kingdom impact will come from the young people you personally disciple. You can impress people from a distance, but you impact them up close. This is the surest way to preserve the fruit of revival. Revival is most fruitful when it has the tracks of personal disciple-making to run on. In the Jesus movement, God raised up leaders like Dawson Trotman, founder of The Navigators, to equip evangelists such as Billy Graham and Bill Bright to be more effective in creating systems and mobilizing laborers to follow up with all of the new believers. If God continues to pour out His Spirit on this generation, ministry leaders must work hard to create wise systems and pray for laborers to multiply, personally discipling all the new believers. Remember: the problem is not with the harvest—the harvest is plentiful. The problem is a lack of laborers (Matt. 9:36–38).

My life was forever changed through a simple process of personal disciple-making. Max Barnett, the director of the University of Oklahoma Baptist Collegiate Ministry, sat down with my twin brother and me at our first meeting and gave us a leather verse pack and a small stack of cards. "Take this card with you everywhere this week and memorize this verse," he said. "I will test you on it next week." I memorized the verse that week, but my main motive was not being the twin that didn't have his verse memorized! After a few weeks of consistent practice, God began a deep, transformative work in my mind and heart. The verses I was memorizing acted like clean water washing a dirty cup (Rom. 12:2). Max had a series of simple training objectives he walked through with us each week—sometimes just a sheet of verses to look up and discuss, sometimes an assignment. Each week built on the previous one. That semester with Max forever changed my life! To this day, when I disciple students, I follow a similar pattern using many of those same simple, reproducible tools. Twenty-one years later, hundreds of people have been discipled by me—or by those I've discipled—continuing the same pattern Max used with me.

Paul commanded Timothy, "and what you have heard from me in the presence of many witnesses entrust to faithful men, who will be able to teach others also" (2 Tim. 2:2). Here we see three spiritual generations, with the implication that there will be many more. Imagine if you led just one person to Christ each year and discipled them to do the same—if this pattern went unbroken, the chain reaction would reach the entire world (over 8 billion people) in just 33 years. Now compare that with a rockstar preacher leading stadiums of 10,000 people to Christ every single day. Even with those incredible results, it would still take more than 2,000 years to reach everyone, and that's without even factoring in population growth! It's clear what our priority should be. Alan Hirsch put it this way: "God can do more with 12 disciples than you can with 1,200 religious consumers."[1] If we focus on the *quality* of our disciple-making, God will take care of the *quantity* of our impact! Dawson Trotman, founder of the Navigators, reminded his leaders, "It's not how many men, but what kind of men."[2]

Large groups and mid-sized small groups are not enough. You must develop a third layer of personal discipleship! You can have the best preaching and programs in the world, but if you are not equipping believers to personally make disciples, your impact will be severely limited. Programs don't make disciples. Disciples make disciples. "Disciples are hand-crafted, not mass produced."[3]

But spiritual depth isn't the only factor. To see multiplication, we must equip every disciple to do personal evangelism. Don't fall into "dead-end discipleship," where Christians just meet with Christians to make them more Christian, and never break out of the Christian subculture. My friend Brian Zunigha says, "Discipleship without evangelism is not discipleship. It's recycle-ship." Too

---

[1] https://quotefancy.com/quote/1789936/Alan-Hirsch-You-can-do-more-with-12-disciples-than-with-1-200-religious-consumers

[2] https://www.challengecsuc.com/assets/pdfs/do-more-with-less-time-by-paul-worcester.pdf

[3] https://discipleship.org/blog/jesus-style-disciple-making/

often, what passes as spiritual multiplication is just reorganizing Christians!

That's why Paul urged Timothy, "But as for you, always be sober-minded, endure suffering, do the work of an evangelist, fulfill your ministry" (2 Tim. 4:5). He reminded Timothy of his own suffering for the gospel: "Therefore I endure everything for the sake of the elect, that they also may obtain the salvation that is in Christ Jesus with eternal glory" (2 Tim. 2:10). Paul used the illustrations of a soldier, athlete, and farmer to stress focus, integrity, and diligence. There's no time for games when eternal souls are at stake (2 Tim. 2:3-7).

The best person to reach a student with the gospel is another student. That is why it is essential that we disciple students well so that they can turn around and reach and disciple others!

Mariana is one of the shyest girls I have ever met. Personally discipled by a leader at Chico State, she developed a heart for the lost and a vision for making disciples. Using a simple strategy we call gospel appointments, she would strike up conversations with new girls at ministry meetings and set up coffee or lunch meetings to go deeper. In these intimate settings, her purpose was clear: hear the other girl's story, share her own, present God's story, and invite a response. Over her college years, this introverted but faithful gospel sharer led over 20 girls to Christ! I remember a few times that she was leading so many people to Christ she had to pass off some of these new believers to others for follow-up. (A good problem to have!) By the time she graduated, some of her disciples had led other girls to Christ, who had then helped other girls find the Lord, representing over 40 girls who were being discipled!

This generation has a hunger to be discipled and make disciples. Let's do our part by praying for and training them up!

Use 2 Timothy 2:1-10 as a guide for your prayers. Ask God to give you at least one young person to disciple and that they will pass it on to others. Pray for a movement of spiritual multiplication among young people in your community and beyond!

Find a supplementary worship-based prayer guide to this chapter in the respective appendix.

Please, also, join us in prayer for this day through the SR App or at strategicrenewal.com/21days

---

CHAPTER 20

SERVANT LEADERSHIP AND SACRIFICE

Dennis Henderson

THE TEACHING AND EXAMPLE of Jesus were always counter-cultural. He did not begin His ministry by proclaiming Himself to be God incarnate. He began to serve and did not seek notoriety. He picked twelve men who, most likely, would not be chosen for a church staff today. They were uneducated, and from what we suspect, were young. His relationships were not with the hierarchy of the religious society. In fact, He publicly called out scribes and Pharisees on several occasions, pointing out their hypocrisy. In Matthew 23:1-10, He stated that they did not practice what they taught, and they desired to sit in the seats of honor to be seen. On multiple occasions, Jesus laid the foundation for leadership. Matthew 19:30 & Mark 10:31 – "But many who are first will be last, and the last first." Matthew 20:26 -27 & Mark 10:43- 44 – "Whoever wants to be great among you must be your servant ... whoever wants to be first must be slave of all." Mark 9:35 – "Anyone who wants to be first must be the very last, and the servant of all." Luke 13:30 – "Indeed, there are those who are last who will be first, and first who will be last." Luke 22:26–27 – "The greatest among you should be like the youngest, and the one who rules like the one who serves... I am among you as one who serves."

Jesus served in the last hours of His life, taking on the role of a servant by washing the disciples' feet. His life as a servant was so clear that the Apostle Paul wrote these words to the Philippian church in the midst of their quarreling: "Let each of you look not only to his own interests, but also to the interests of others. Have this mind among yourselves, which is yours in Christ Jesus, who, though he was in the form of God, did not count equality with God a thing to be grasped, but emptied himself, by taking the form of a servant, being born in the likeness of men. And being found in human form, he humbled himself by becoming obedient to the point of death, even death on a cross" (Phil. 2:4-8).

One of Jesus' strongest statements concerning His life is found in Matthew 20:27-28 – " and whoever would be first among you must be your slave, even as the Son of Man came not to be served but to serve, and to give his life as a ransom for many." He doubles down on the statement as he dealt with James and John wanting to sit next to Him in the coming kingdom. Mark 10:42-45 – " Jesus called them together and said, 'You know that those who are regarded as rulers of the Gentiles lord it over them, and their high officials exercise authority over them. Not so with you. Instead, whoever wants to become great among you must be your servant, and whoever wants to be first must be slave of all. For even the Son of Man did not come to be served, but to serve, and to give his life as a ransom for many.' " I am sure it was shocking for them to hear this. Although the Old Testament provided many examples of leaders who prioritized serving others over themselves, the disciples lived in a world heavily influenced by the Romans, who viewed people as slaves and servants. Moses, David, Nehemiah,

Ezra, and many more sought the good of the people and sacrificed for them. But the heavy shadow of the Romans darkened the eyes of the twelve as Jesus corrected them by His statements of inverted leadership.

We are not just called to serve. As believers, it is who we are. We are servants. It is not an activity we carry out at church or in the neighborhood—it is the core of our being. We are servants, and with it come some principles. One thing that we must have as our baseline is that Jesus owns us, and we are not our own. We are not the masters of our ship. Paul makes this clear in 1 Corinthians 6:19-20 – "Or do you not know that your body is a temple of the Holy Spirit within you, whom you have from God? You are not your own, for you were bought with a price. So, glorify God in your body." This is not always clear to many as they follow Jesus. In a culture where it is taught and displayed that we have rights and no one can invade those rights, it is difficult for them to accept this.

A second principle that accompanies the concept of servant leadership is that it comes at a cost. The cost is a sacrifice. We do not go out to find a lamb to sacrifice, but we pay the price in time, money, energy, humility, and ridicule. We yield our plans to others. Jesus said on more than one occasion, "If anyone would come after me, let him deny himself and take up his cross daily and follow me" (Luke 9:23).

Servant leadership is rare, but it is the gold standard for a Christ follower. The way forward is to start at the end of the line. This day, thank Jesus for His marvelous service to us through His sacrifice on the cross. Let the Scriptures you've just read be your guide, and also as you pray for the next generation. Thank Him for washing feet, healing the sick, dining with sinners, and becoming one of us. Thank Him for the cross, the ultimate price of dying for you. Then respond. It might be a moment of confession that you haven't yet become a humble servant to others for the sake of the gospel. Then move forward, seeking to be like the Savior who served and sacrificed everything for you.

Find a supplementary worship-based prayer guide to this chapter in the respective appendix.

Please, also, join us in prayer for this day through the SR App or at strategicrenewal.com/21days

---

CHAPTER 21

A GENERATION SET APART FOR GOD

Thai Lam

> *"In the third year of the reign of Jehoiakim king of Judah, Nebuchadnezzar king of Babylon came to Jerusalem and besieged it... Then the king commanded Ashpenaz, his chief eunuch, to bring some of the people of Israel, both of the royal family and of the nobility, youths without blemish, of good appearance and skillful in all wisdom, endowed with knowledge, understanding learning, and competent to stand in the king's palace, and to teach them the literature and language of the Chaldeans. The king assigned them a daily portion of the food that the king ate, and of the wine that he drank. They were to be educated for three years, and at the end of that time, they were to stand before the king" (Dan. 1:1,3-5 ESV).*

In the days of Nebuchadnezzar and Israel's exile to Babylon, four Jewish teenagers, Daniel, Hananiah, Mishael, and Azariah, are brought into Nebuchadnezzar's school of leadership to be trained in the language and pagan literature of Babylon. Part of the training was a daily regimen of the king's choice foods. What was Nebuchadnezzar's objective in taking a handful of young leaders from a slave nation and giving them a full-ride scholarship to Babylon's "Ivy League" university—including room and board in the king's palace and dining hall? I think Nebuchadnezzar desired to cultivate an appetite in these future leaders for Babylonian comforts and pleasures, to erode their resolve to preserve Jewish heritage and their zeal to be set apart according to Jewish law, and to dull their resistance through imbibing the spirit and culture of Babylon.

> *"Among these were Daniel, Hananiah, Mishael, and Azariah of the tribe of Judah. And the chief of the eunuchs gave them names: Daniel he called Belteshazzar, Hananiah he called Shadrach, Mishael he called Meshach, and Azariah he called Abednego. But Daniel resolved that he would not defile himself with the king's food, or with the wine that he drank. Therefore he asked the chief of the eunuchs to allow him not to defile himself" (Dan. 1:6-8 ESV).*

With their admission to the University of Babylon, these four Jewish teenagers were also given Babylonian names: Daniel, whose name means "God is my judge," is renamed Belteshazzar, meaning "Lady, protect the King"; Hananiah ("Yahweh has been gracious") is renamed Shadrach ("I am fear of god"); Mishael ("Who is what God is?") is renamed Meshach ("I am despised, contemptible, humiliated"); and Azariah ("Yahweh has helped") is renamed Abednego ("Servant of Nebo"). Nebuchadnezzar wanted to redefine their identity.

Like Nebuchadnezzar in Babylon, Satan, in the modern context of our secular and humanistic universities, desires to dull our zeal for holiness and wholeheartedness to Jesus and to erode our resistance to the lust of the eyes, the lust of the flesh, and the pride of life. The same holy prescription applies to college students and young adults today as it did for Daniel and his comrades in the days of Babylon: these young leaders gave themselves to a consecrated lifestyle of fasting and prayer.

> *"At the end of ten days it was seen that they were better in appearance and fatter in flesh than all the youths who ate the king's food. So the steward took away their food and the wine they were to drink, and gave them vegetables. As for these four youths, God gave them learning and skill in all literature and wisdom, and Daniel had understanding in all visions and dreams. At the end of the time, when the king had commanded that they should be brought in, the chief of the eunuchs brought them in before Nebuchadnezzar. And the king spoke with them, and among all of them none was found like Daniel, Hananiah, Mishael, and Azariah. Therefore they stood before the king. And in every matter of wisdom and understanding about which the king inquired of them, he found them ten times better than all the magicians and enchanters that were in all his kingdom" (Dan. 1:15-20 ESV).*

They voluntarily chose to forego the pleasures of the king's fine dining and embraced a prayerful lifestyle of fasting on vegetables for the three years they were at the University of Babylon. In learning to refuse the legitimate pleasures of food, favor, and comfort, they grew in grace and strength to refuse the illegitimate pleasures of compromise, pleasing man, and selfish ambition. By allowing the Lord to operate on the appetites of their bellies through a lifestyle of fasting and prayer, God set them apart and gave them "learning and skill in all literature and wisdom" TEN times better than their peers, and they became leaders in Babylon with understanding from heaven that shifted history.

May the Lord do it again in our day! Let's pray for this next generation to be a generation set apart for God!

1. Pray that God would set apart youth like Daniel, Hananiah, Mishael, and Azariah from an early age with a hunger and zeal for God, with their identities rooted in Christ, who would be fully surrendered to His purposes in their generation.

2. Pray for God to raise up young leaders who would set their hearts to grow in love and intimacy with God, in a lifestyle of fasting and prayer, and in wisdom and understanding of God's ways.

3. Pray for revival amongst teens, college students, young adults, and prodigals who grew up in the Church, and for spiritual awakening amongst the lost, the broken, and the hurting who have yet to encounter Jesus.

Find a supplementary worship-based prayer guide to this chapter in the respective appendix.

Please, also, join us in prayer for this day through the SR App or at strategicrenewal.com/21days

CONCLUSION
AS THE STUDENTS GO, SO GOES THE NATION

We live with a rich history of spiritual awakening. From the earliest days of the Church's birth in Acts 2, to the Apostle Paul's remarkable missionary journeys, the desert fathers and mothers, and the expansive spread of the gospel throughout the Roman Empire. Later reform movements, such as the monastic renewal in the 12th century and the Protestant Reformation of the 16th century, stand out as beacons of light amidst dark cultural backdrops. Additionally, North America experienced at least two notable Great Awakenings in the 18th and 19th centuries, catalyzing a revival of repentance, purity, love, service, evangelism, and discipleship, which resulted in extraordinary impact across the globe.

Yet it was out of the Second Great Awakening (1790-1845) that many across North America began hosting monthly concerts of prayer for almost half a century! During this extraordinary movement, church leaders began to focus the power of united prayer on the needs of college students. It is recorded that "by 1815, the Concert of Prayer for Colleges had become a regular feature on the New England campuses of Yale, Williams, Brown, and Middlebury. By 1823, almost every major denomination and university in America had embraced the practice of a concerted day of prayer for colleges."[1] A majority of American churches embraced the conviction that college students contained the future of their congregations as disciples engaging in culture and impacting society as the salt and light of Christ. Essentially, they correlated the spiritual climate of college communities to the future climate of the country, saying, "as the students go, so goes the nation."[2]

In his *Handbook of Revivals*, Henry C. Fish gives us an astonishing account of the ongoing success of this special day of prayer. He says, *"In the year 1823, the last Thursday of February each year was agreed upon as the day for special supplication that God would pour from on high His Spirit upon our Colleges and Seminaries. And what have been some of the results? In the years 1824 and 1825, revivals were experienced in 5 different colleges; in 1826, in 6 colleges; in 1831, in 19... In one of the colleges, it is stated that a revival started on the very day of the concert of prayer. In 1835, not less than 18 revivals were reported by different colleges."*[3]

Since 2016, there has been a renewed emphasis on highlighting the last Thursday of February each year for the church to focus its prayers on colleges and universities, not only in North America but across the world. Two hundred years ago, there were only 200 universities around which the church united in prayer. As of 2026, there are over 3,200 four-year universities, not counting the myriad of two-year college institutions and trade schools.

Jesus said in Luke 10:2 that "the harvest is plentiful, but the la-

---

[1] https://collegiatedayofprayer.org/about/history/

[2] Ibid

[3] Ibid.

borers are few." College and university campuses are a rich harvest. It was true 200 years ago, and it is still true today. Only, may the laborers not be few anymore, but many! May these past 21 days of united prayer produce in you a fresh movement and lifestyle of worship-based intercession for the next generation! And may the future of pastors committed to prayer and Word-powered ministry (Acts 6:4), and disciples of good repute, full of the Spirit and wisdom (Acts 6:3), be paved through the united prayers of the people like you and me, so that we will again see another great movement of God towards the completion of the Great Commission (Acts 6:7)!

APPENDIX
WORSHIP-BASED PRAYER GUIDES

The following prayer guides are intended to supplement each chapter and guide you into deeper intercession for the next generation. Each guide highlights a key passage mentioned or alluded to in their corresponding chapter and will be especially helpful not only in individual times of intercession but also within the context of communal prayer. Each guide follows the 4/4 pattern of prayer, which is an application of the way Jesus commanded and modeled for us to pray. If this pattern of prayer is new to you, please refer to https://strategicrenewal.com/worshipbasedprayer/ to read more.

Spiritual Fathers, Mothers, and Grandparents Prayer Guide

Psalm 145: 1-7

REVERENCE – *Identify and celebrate God's praiseworthy attributes*

- God is King (v. 1)
- He is worthy of eternal praise (vv. 1-2)
- God is great and His greatness is unsearchable (v. 3)
- Lord over all generations and mighty (v. 4)
- Glorious and majestic (v. 5)
- He is wondrous, awesome, abundantly good, and righteous (vv. 5-7)

Prayer Prompts

- God, I extol You as King over... (v. 1)
- Lord, I will bless You forever and ever because Your name is... (v. 1)
- Lord, Your greatness has been displayed in every generation by... (v.3)

RESPONSE – *Surrender to Him and His ways*

- Lord, I confess that instead of meditating on Your majesty, I focus on... (v. 5)
- God my King, I admit that I lack a multigenerational perspective in... (v. 4)

REQUESTS – *Ask the Spirit to guide prayer over concerns, resources, and relationships*

- Lord, open my eyes to see the next generation around me so that... (v. 4)
- God, may the next generation hear the proclamation that You can... (v. 4)
- Lord, may the next generation declare Your greatness by... (v. 6)

READINESS – *Encouragement and strength for spiritual battle*

- Great God, reveal Your abundant goodness, especially as the next generation faces... (v. 7)
- Raise up a song of Your righteousness to be sung by Your multigenerational Church as we... (v. 7)

Identity in Christ Prayer Guide

2 Corinthians 5:17-21

REVERENCE – *Identify and celebrate God's praiseworthy attributes*

- Makes us new (v. 17)
- He is the Reconciler (vv. 18-20)
- He is merciful, not counting our sins against us (v. 19)
- He is our gracious substitute for sin (v. 21)
- He is righteous and able to make us righteous (v.21)

Prayer Prompts

- I praise You, Lord, that because I am new in Christ… (v. 17)
- God, I worship You for reconciling me to Yourself even when… (v. 18)
- Lord, thank You for making Your appeal of reconciliation to me through… (v.20)

RESPONSE – *Surrender to Him and His ways*

- Lord, even though I am a new creation, I confess my struggle of basing my identity on… (v. 17)
- God, I admit that I've not embraced my call as Your ambassador when… (v. 20)

REQUESTS – *Ask the Spirit to guide prayer over concerns, resources, and relationships*

- Lord, help the next generation fully realize and trust their identity in Christ so that… (v. 17)
- God, help me embrace my calling as Your ambassador to the next generation, especially to… (vv. 18, 20)
- Jesus, may the next generation be reconciled to __________ in order that… (v. 19)

READINESS – *Encouragement and strength for spiritual battle*

- Lord, remind the next generation that they are reconciled to Christ, especially when the enemy tries to… (v. 18)
- Jesus, may younger generations display righteous character in the face of… (v. 20)

Purpose and Calling Prayer Guide

Ephesians 2:8-10

REVERENCE – *Identify and celebrate God's praiseworthy attributes*

- God is a gracious Savior (v. 8)
- Gives us the gift of faith (v. 8)
- He is worthy of our boasting (v.9)
- He is our Creator (v. 10)
- He providentially prepares good works (v. 10)

Prayer Prompts

- God, I praise You for showing me Your grace when… (v. 8)
- Jesus, I worship You for saving me from… (v. 8)
- Jesus, I boast in You because… (v.9)
- Lord, thank You for Your grace that has saved me for… (v.10)

RESPONSE – *Surrender to Him and His ways*

- Lord, I acknowledge that I still try to earn Your favor by… (v. 8)
- Jesus, I repent of boasting in my work of… (v. 9)

REQUESTS – *Ask the Spirit to guide prayer over concerns, resources, and relationships*

- Lord, may Your grace empower (*name*) towards their purpose of... (vv. 8,10)
- God, please give the next generation discernment to know the good works You've prepared for them as they... (v. 10)
- Jesus, help the next generation to work from a place of intimacy with You, especially in... (vv. 8-9)

READINESS – *Encouragement and strength for spiritual battle*

- Remind (*name*) of the gift of Your grace as they battle against... (v. 8)
- Jesus, empower the next generation as Your workmanship to overcome... (v. 10)

Holiness in a Hostile Culture Prayer Guide
John 17:14-19

REVERENCE – *Identify and celebrate God's praiseworthy attributes*

- Giver of the Word (v. 14)
- Keeps and protects us (v. 15)
- Jesus is holy, not of this world (v.16)
- He is the Sanctifier of our souls (v. 17)
- He is the one who sets us apart and sends us (v. 18)

Prayer Prompts

- Father, thank You for giving us Your Word that says... (v. 14)
- Jesus, I praise You for sanctifying me in Your truth so that... (v. 17)
- I worship You, Jesus, that You are able to protect me from... (v.15)
- Father, I praise You for sending Jesus into the world to... (v.18)

RESPONSE – *Surrender to Him and His ways*

- Jesus, forgive me for giving in to the ways of the world when... (v. 14)
- Father, I admit I've neglected Your call towards holiness in the way I... (v. 17)

REQUESTS – *Ask the Spirit to guide prayer over concerns, resources, and relationships*

- Lord Jesus, set apart the next generation in Your truth so that... (v. 17)
- Father, help (*name*) receive Your Word so that they can endure the hostility of... (vv. 14-15)
- Jesus, because You have consecrated Yourself, may the next generation courageously carry Your holy Word to... (vv.18-19)

READINESS – *Encouragement and strength for spiritual battle*

- Jesus, please keep the next generation from the evil of... (v. 15)
- Lord, sanctify us in the truth to be victorious over... (v. 19)

Developing Praying Leaders Prayer Guide

Mark 11:15-19

REVERENCE – *Identify and celebrate God's praiseworthy attributes*

- Displays righteous anger (v. 15)
- Purifies the purposes of the temple (v. 15)
- Cleanses distraction and competition for our devotion (v. 16)
- The authoritative owner of the temple (v. 16, 17)
- Teacher of truth and fulfiller of Scripture (v.17)
- Makes a way for all nations to be in relationship with Him (v. 19)
- To be feared (v. 18)

Prayer Prompts

- Jesus, I praise You for having authority over... (vv. 16-17)
- Jesus, I worship You for teaching me the truth about prayer that... (v. 17)
- I reverence You, Lord, because... (v.18)
- Jesus, I am astonished and amazed that You... (v.18)

RESPONSE – *Surrender to Him and His ways*

- Jesus, drive out my distractions with __________ and restore the priority of prayer in my life. (vv. 16-17)
- Lord, enter *this* temple and purify my false motives in.... (v. 17)

REQUESTS – *Ask the Spirit to guide prayer over concerns, resources, and relationships*

- Lord, restore the place of prayer in my __________ (*list areas of life you are not seeking God*). (v.13)
- Jesus, help the Church prioritize prayer so that the next generation will... (v. 17)
- Lord, please help me teach the next generation that... (vv. 17-18)

READINESS – *Encouragement and strength for spiritual battle*

- Jesus, help me overcome the opposition of _________ as I seek to make prayer the central activity of my life. (v. 17)
- Lord, lead me this week in cultivating the priority of prayer in/at __________ (*list areas of influence, leadership, or service*). (vv.15-17)

Gospel Partnerships Prayer Guide

Philippians 1:3-6

REVERENCE – *Identify and celebrate God's praiseworthy attributes*

- God of remembrance and joy (vv. 3-4)
- Works through partnership to advance the gospel (v. 5)
- God of assurance (v. 6)
- God is the beginner and completer of all good work (v. 6)

Prayer Prompts

- Father, I thank You that I'm filled with joy when I remember... (vv. 3-4)
- Jesus, I praise You that prayer brings joy because... (v. 4)
- Lord Jesus, I worship You as the one who has begun and will complete the good work of... (v. 6)

RESPONSE – *Surrender to Him and His ways*

- Lord, I confess I do not remember to bring __________ to you in prayer. Help me to be joyfully consistent to pray for... (v. 3)
- Lord, I admit that I often try to do Your work on my own rather than partnering with others, especially when... (v. 5)

REQUESTS – *Ask the Spirit to guide prayer over concerns, resources, and relationships*

- Jesus, bring Your assurance to the next generation...
  - ...that You have __________ (good work God has done).
  - ...that You are __________ (good work God is doing).
  - ...that You will __________ (good work God will do). (v. 6)
- God as I remember (*name*) now, I pray for a renewed partnership in the gospel so that... (v. 5)

READINESS – *Encouragement and strength for spiritual battle*

- Jesus, remind the next generation that they're not alone in the gospel work of... (vv. 4-5)
- Lord, because You're faithful to finish what You start, guard the next generation from being discouraged about... (v. 6)

Legacy-Minded Churches Prayer Guide

Psalm 78:1-7

REVERENCE – *Identify and celebrate God's praiseworthy attributes*

- He teaches and reveals (vv. 1-2)
- He is the God of glorious deeds, might, and wonder (v. 5)
- Establishes testimony and law to be observed and taught (v. 5)
- He is the God of all generations (v. 6)
- God of hope for all (v. 7)

Prayer Prompts

- God, I praise You for Your glorious deed of... (v. 4)
- Thank You for demonstrating Your mighty wonders in my life by... (v. 4)
- Lord, I am so grateful for (*name*), who told me about how You... (vv. 4-5)

RESPONSE – *Surrender to Him and His ways*

- Forgive me for failing to teach (*name*) about Your ways so they would put their hope in You! (vv. 4, 6)
- Lord, I confess often forgetting Your work of __________, and I recommit my life now to keep Your life-giving commands. (v. 7)

REQUESTS – *Ask the Spirit to guide prayer over concerns, resources, and relationships*

- Lord, please give me a vision and ability to teach (*name*) about Your wonders and might. (v.4)
- Help us, Lord, to be intentional in relationally discipling the next generation by... (vv. 5-6)
- Lord, in Your might, give me a legacy mindset to dream that a generation yet to be born will one day... (.v. 6)

READINESS – *Encouragement and strength for spiritual battle*

- Oh God of all generations, help us not to forget Your works, even when we face... (v..7)
- Lord, give the next generation hope to overcome... (v. 7)

Authentic Relationships Prayer Guide

Ephesians 4:29-32

REVERENCE – *Identify and celebrate God's praiseworthy attributes*

- Giver of grace (v. 29)
- God the Holy Spirit is personal and relational (v. 30)
- He is our sealer and redeemer (v. 30)
- God is kind and tenderhearted (v. 32)
- Forgiving (v. 32)

Prayer Prompts

- God, I praise You for the grace You gave through the words of (*name*), who builds me up by... (v. 29)
- Holy Spirit, thank You for sealing me to be redeemed from... (v. 30)
- Jesus, I worship You for showing me kindness and forgiveness, especially when... (v. 32)

RESPONSE – *Surrender to Him and His ways*

- God, I repent of grieving the Holy Spirit when I used words to __________ instead of building up. (vv. 29-30)
- I confess my bitterness and anger over... (v. 31)
- Jesus, forgive me for not being kind, tenderhearted, and forgiving towards [*name*] when they... (v. 32)

REQUESTS – *Ask the Spirit to guide prayer over concerns, resources, and relationships*

- Jesus, please help the next generation cultivate authentic relationships by… (vv. 29, 32)
- God, help students across our country to build up others in Your grace through the way they… (v. 29)
- Father, help the local church of __________ to demonstrate kindness and tender hearts to the next generation so that… (v. 32)

READINESS – *Encouragement and strength for spiritual battle*

- Lord Jesus, may Your grace overcome our temptation towards superficial relationships when… (v. 29)
- Father, keep us from grieving the Holy Spirit, especially when we're tempted to… (v. 30)

Loneliness, Depression, and Anxiety Prayer Guide

Matthew 4:1-11

REVERENCE – *Identify and celebrate God's praiseworthy attributes*

- God the Holy Spirit is our leader (v. 1)
- Jesus is the Son of God (v. 3)
- His Word is our most important sustenance (v. 4)
- His Word is our ultimate authority (vv. 4, 7, 10)
- He alone is worthy of our worship (v. 32)

Prayer Prompts

- God, thank You for leading me when… (v. 1)
- God, I praise You for how Your Word sustains me, especially when… (v. 4)
- Jesus, I worship You for Your humble authority over… (v. 7)
- Lord, I worship You alone because… (v. 10)

RESPONSE – *Surrender to Him and His ways*

- God, I confess that in times of temptation, I often rely on __________ instead of Your authoritative Word. (vv. 4, 7, 10)
- Jesus, I admit that I tend to hunger after __________ rather than Your sustaining Word. (v. 4)

REQUESTS – *Ask the Spirit to guide prayer over concerns, resources, and relationships*

- Jesus, as the next generation battles against anxiety and loneliness, remind them that Your Word says... (v. 4)
- God, help us to draw closer to the next generation so that... (v. 11)
- Holy Spirit, lead students and test them so that their faith will be victorious over... (vv. 1, 11)

READINESS – *Encouragement and strength for spiritual battle*

- Lord Jesus, when the next generation is tempted with comfort and power, help them obey Your Word, that says... (vv. 4, 7, 10)
- Father, when students face depression, strengthen them to depend on You for... (v. 4, 7)

Digital Discernment and Social Media Engagement Prayer Guide

Philippians 4:8-9

REVERENCE – *Identify and celebrate God's praiseworthy attributes*

- God is the standard of truth and whatever is honorable, just, pure, lovely, commendable, and excellent (v. 8)
- He is worthy of praise! (v.8)
- God of peace (v. 9)

Prayer Prompts

- God, I praise You for how I have experienced Your (*majesty, justice, purity, love, excellence*) when... (v. 8)
- Lord, You are worthy of my praise and full attention because... (v. 8)
- God, thank You for giving me peace when I was facing... (v. 9)

RESPONSE – *Surrender to Him and His ways*

- God, I surrender my tendency to focus on __________ instead of what is true and honorable. (v. 8)
- Jesus, I confess that I often forsake the peace You give when I allow my mind to be consumed with... (vv. 8-9)

REQUESTS – *Ask the Spirit to guide prayer over concerns, resources, and relationships*

- Lord, may the next generation be guided by what is true, honorable, just, pure, lovely, and commendable as they... (v. 8)
- God, please give the next generation discernment in their engagement with social media and technology so that... (v. 9)
- God, empower students with wisdom to leverage digital platforms to bring the gospel to... (vv. 8-9)
- God, may Your peace be with the next generation as they practice... (v. 9)

READINESS – *Encouragement and strength for spiritual battle*

- Lord, may Your peace protect the minds of students, especially when... (v. 9)
- Father, may the next generation be marked by your purity and love so that the enemy's attempt to use social media to __________ would be overthrown. (v. 8)

Building a Biblical Worldview Prayer Guide

Colossian 3:1-4

REVERENCE – *Identify and celebrate God's praiseworthy attributes*

- Jesus is our resurrected Lord (v. 1)
- Seated at God's right hand in power and authority (v.1)
- Eternal and everlasting (v. 2)
- He is the keeper and sustainer of life (v. 3)
- Glorious (v. 4)

Prayer Prompts

- God, I praise You that because I've been raised with Christ, then... (v. 1)
- Jesus, since You are seated at God's right hand, You have power and authority over... (v. 1)
- God, thank You for giving me Your perspective when... (v. 2)
- Father, I worship You that in Christ, I am dead to __________ and now alive towards __________. (v. 3)

RESPONSE – *Surrender to Him and His ways*

- God, I confess that I often view the world through __________ rather than from your perspective. (vv. 1-2)
- Jesus, forgiving me for setting my mind on __________ when it comes to... (v. 2)

REQUESTS – *Ask the Spirit to guide prayer over concerns, resources, and relationships*

- Lord, help the next generation seek the things that are above so that... (v.1)
- God, set our minds to have Your view on the next generation so that... (v. 2)
- Jesus, give us Your insight to see how the Church can help students build a biblical worldview, especially concerning... (vv. 3-4)

READINESS – *Encouragement and strength for spiritual battle*

- Jesus, remind us that You are seated at the right hand of God and give us victory over the enemy's scheme of... (v. 1)
- Christ, who is our life, give Your Church an eternal perspective as we face... (v. 4)

Resisting Cultural Conformity Prayer Guide

Romans 12:1-2

REVERENCE – *Identify and celebrate God's praiseworthy attributes*

- Merciful (v. 1)
- Holy (v. 1)
- He is the renewer of our mind (v. 2)
- He is good and perfect (v. 2)

Prayer Prompts

- God, I praise You for showing me Your mercies, especially when… (v. 1)
- Lord, You are worthy of my sacrifice of… (v. 1)
- Thank You for transforming and renewing my mind by… (v. 2)
- God, I worship You for Your good and perfect will for… (v. 2)

RESPONSE – *Surrender to Him and His ways*

- God, I confess that I have taken Your mercy for granted when… (v. 1)
- I repent of being conformed to the world by… (v. 2)

REQUESTS – *Ask the Spirit to guide prayer over concerns, resources, and relationships*

- God, give Your mercy to the next generation so that... (v. 1)
- Help students to present their bodies as living sacrifices by... (v. 1)
- Empower the next generation to worship You by serving... (v. 1)
- Jesus, transform and renew the minds of young people so that they will know and trust Your perfect will for... (v. 2)

READINESS – *Encouragement and strength for spiritual battle*

- God, may Your mercy enable students to resist the worldly conformity of... (v. 1)
- Lord, transform and renew the minds of the next generation in order to overcome... (v. 2)

Courageous Faith in Crisis and Suffering Prayer Guide

1 Peter 1:3-7

REVERENCE – *Identify and celebrate God's praiseworthy attributes*

- God of great mercy (v. 3)
- Our living hope and resurrected Lord (v. 3)
- Powerfully guards us (v. 5)
- Savior (v. 5)
- Source of joy (v. 6)
- Worthy of all praise, glory, and honor (v. 7)

Prayer Prompts

- God, I praise You for showing me the greatness of Your mercy when... (v. 3)
- Jesus, because You were raised from the dead, I can have hope for... (v. 3)
- Lord, I rejoice even though... (v. 6)
- God, I give You praise, glory, and honor because... (v. 7)

RESPONSE – *Surrender to Him and His ways*

- Father, I confess that I struggle to have joy in the midst of my grief about... (v. 6)
- Lord Jesus, I surrender my current trial of ... (v. 6)

REQUESTS – *Ask the Spirit to guide prayer over concerns, resources, and relationships*

- Jesus, because You are our living hope, help the next generation to rejoice when they face (*list specific trials*). (v. 6)
- God, may the faith of students at __________ be found genuine so that... (v. 7)
- Lord, please strengthen the next generation as they endure the crisis of... (v. 1)
- Help students to embrace Your sovereign role of suffering so that... (vv. 6-7)

READINESS – *Encouragement and strength for spiritual battle*

- God, please guard the next generation in Your power, especially as they encounter... (vv. 5-6)
- Lord Jesus, may Your hope encourage the next generation to reflect You well in their trials of... (v. 7)

Spirit-filled Living Prayer Guide

Ephesians 5:15-21

REVERENCE – *Identify and celebrate God's praiseworthy attributes*

- Source of wisdom and provider of time (vv. 15-16)
- His will is understandable (v. 18)
- His Spirit fills us (v. 18)
- He is worthy of our heartfelt singing (v.19)
- He is our Father and Lord (v. 20)
- He is to be revered! (v. 21)

Prayer Prompts

- Lord, I thank You that when I am filled with the Holy Spirit, then... (v. 18)
- Lord, thank You that Your will can be understood about... (v. 17)
- Lord, I rejoice even though... (v. 6)
- God, I give You praise, glory, and honor because... (v. 7)

RESPONSE – *Surrender to Him and His ways*

- I confess that I have not walked in wisdom and been foolish when... (vv. 15-16)
- Father, I admit my misunderstanding of the Holy Spirit concerning... (vv. 17-18)
- I repent of often being filled by (controlled by) __________ instead of the Holy Spirit when... (v. 18)

REQUESTS – *Ask the Spirit to guide prayer over concerns, resources, and relationships*

- Father, help the next generation continually receive the filling of the Holy Spirit, so that... (v. 18)
- God, help students to trust the Holy Spirit's power for... (v. 18)
- Jesus, help us as the Church to accurately teach the next generation that the Holy Spirit... (v. 19)
- Help the Church model a Spirit-filled life by... (vv. 19-21)

READINESS – *Encouragement and strength for spiritual battle*

- Out of reverence for Christ, help us to walk in submission to the Holy Spirit and others, especially when... (v. 21)
- Empower the next generation to model Spirit-filled living as they face... (vv. 18-21)

Marks of a True Move of God Prayer Guide

Romans 12:9-21

REVERENCE – *Identify and celebrate God's praiseworthy attributes*

- He is the God of genuine love (v. 9)
- He is good (v. 9)
- He is worthy of our zealous and fervent service (v. 11)
- Source of joy and hope (v. 12)
- God of just wrath and vengeance (v. 19)
- Overcomes evil (v. 21)

Prayer Prompts

- Lord, I praise You for how I experienced Your genuine love when... (v. 9)
- Thank You that we can rejoice in hope today because... (v. 12)
- God, I worship You for overcoming... (v. 21)

RESPONSE – *Surrender to Him and His ways*

- Lord, I repent for not loving my Christian brothers and sisters by failing to... (v. 10)
- Father, I am sorry for not doing my part in living peaceably with (*name*). Help us to live in harmony! (vv. 16,18)

REQUESTS – *Ask the Spirit to guide prayer over concerns, resources, and relationships*

- We pray that the next generation would be marked by __________ (*choose a description of genuine love*) so that... (vv. 9-18)
- Lord, we pray for Your work on the campus of __________ (*list a college/university*), that You would... (vv. 9-18)
- Jesus, help the local church fervently serve the next generation by... (v. 11)

READINESS – *Encouragement and strength for spiritual battle*

- Lord, help us hold fast to what is good today so that the evil of __________ would be overcome! (vv. 9, 21)

Antiphonal Response

Men: "Do not be overcome by evil!"
Women: "But overcome evil with good!"

Gospel Boldness and Witness Prayer Guide

Acts 4:23-31

REVERENCE – *Identify and celebrate God's praiseworthy attributes*

- Sovereign Lord (v. 24)
- Creator of all (v. 24)
- Speaks through His Holy Spirit and Word (v. 25)
- Predestines and fulfills plans (v. 28)
- Sees and knows all (v. 29)
- Powerful healer (v. 30)
- Holy servant (v. 30)

Prayer Prompts

- Lord, I praise You as Sovereign over... (v. 24)
- Thank you, Lord, for the wisdom of Your Word that says... (v. 25)
- God, You alone have power and authority to accomplish Your plans for... (v. 28)

RESPONSE – *Surrender to Him and His ways*

- Lord, because You're sovereign, we surrender __________ to You. (v. 24)
- Help us to trust Your hand and gospel plan even though... (vv. 27-28)

REQUESTS – *Ask the Spirit to guide prayer over concerns, resources, and relationships*

- Lord, as You look upon the next generation, give them boldness to... (v. 29)
- Lord, stretch out Your sovereign hand to reveal Jesus to students by... (v. 30)
- Jesus, bring Your healing power to (*name*) so that... (v. 30)

READINESS – *Encouragement and strength for spiritual battle*

- Sovereign Lord, fill the next generation with the Holy Spirit to overcome... (v. 31)
- Holy Spirit, fill us today so that we will speak Your Word boldly to... (v. 31)

Global Vision and Missional Heart Prayer Guide

Acts 1:8

REVERENCE – *Identify and celebrate God's praiseworthy attributes*

- Powerful
- Promise keeper
- Global heart
- Strategic

Prayer Prompts

- Father, I exalt You that because You kept Your promise to send the Holy Spirit, ...
- Thank you, Jesus, that (*name*) was a Spirit-empowered witness to me when...
- Holy Spirit, I praise You because Your power can...

RESPONSE – *Surrender to Him and His ways*

- Father, forgive me for not relying on the Spirit's power in my witness to (*name*).
- Lord, I confess that I have been shortsighted in Your mission when...

REQUESTS – *Ask the Spirit to guide prayer over concerns, resources, and relationships*

- Father, may the next generation receive the promised Holy Spirit so that...
- Jesus, bring the gospel to __________ through this next generation!
- Holy Spirit, empower students to be Jesus' witness on their campus by...

READINESS – *Encouragement and strength for spiritual battle*

- Lord Jesus, may the Holy Spirit empower our witness to You even when...
- Help us overcome the enemy's attempt to keep us self-focused by...

Revival and Awakening Prayer Guide

Revelation 2:1-7

REVERENCE – *Identify and celebrate God's praiseworthy attributes*

- Jesus is in charge of all leaders and churches (v. 1)
- He knows our works and our struggles (vv. 2-3)
- Worthy of our first love (v. 4)
- Lovingly and justly disciplines and judges (v. 5)
- Rewarder of obedience (v. 7)

Prayer Prompts

- Jesus, You alone are worthy of our first love because... (v. 4)
- Lord Jesus, I praise You that You are in charge of __________ (*list specific leaders and churches*). (v. 1)
- Jesus, I am so grateful that You know and care about my work/struggle of... (vv. 2-3)

RESPONSE – *Surrender to Him and His ways*

- Jesus, I repent of devoting myself to the lesser love of... (v. 4)
- Lord, I confess that I lack patient endurance with... (v. 3)

REQUESTS – *Ask the Spirit to guide prayer over concerns, resources, and relationships*

- Father, revive the next generation of Christians to their first love in Jesus so that... (v. 4)
- Lord Jesus, awaken (*list specific students*) to the gospel in order that... (v. 5)
- Help the Church to join You in Your work of __________ in the next generation! (v. 7)

READINESS – *Encouragement and strength for spiritual battle*

- Jesus, help the next generation hear and obey the Holy Spirit so that they can conquer... (v. 7)
- Lord, as we join You in Your work, help us not to grow weary, especially when... (v. 3)

Multiplication of Disciple-Makers Prayer Guide

2 Timothy 2:1-10

REVERENCE – *Identify and celebrate God's praiseworthy attributes*

- Gracious (v. 1)
- Faithfully suffered (v. 3)
- Gives understanding (v. 7)
- Risen from the dead (v. 8)
- Eternally glorious (v. 10)

Prayer Prompts

- Jesus, I praise You for strengthening me in Your grace when... (v. 1)
- Lord Jesus, thank You for (*someone who discipled you*), who You brought into my life to... (v. 2)
- Jesus, I worship You that because You have risen from the dead... (v. 10)

RESPONSE – *Surrender to Him and His ways*

- I admit that I have not been faithful to teach... (v. 2)
- Lord, I confess my struggle with suffering for You when... (vv. 3, 9)

REQUESTS – *Ask the Spirit to guide prayer over concerns, resources, and relationships*

- Jesus, we pray that the next generation would be greatly strengthened in Your grace so that… (v. 1)
- Christ Jesus, may resilient disciples be multiplied at __________ (*name specific colleges and universities*). (v. 2)
- Help us, Lord Jesus, to faithfully preach the gospel to __________ (*name specific students*) in order that… (v. 8)

Antiphonal Response: "The word of God is not bound!"

- Give us understanding to raise up disciple-makers at __________ (*name your local church*) in order to reach… (v. 7)

READINESS – *Encouragement and strength for spiritual battle*

- Jesus, may Your grace help the next generation to share in suffering by… (v. 3)
- Make it our aim to please You alone today, even as we're tempted to… (v. 4)

Servant Leadership and Sacrifice Prayer Guide

Philippians 2:1-11

REVERENCE – *Identify and celebrate God's praiseworthy attributes*

- Encourager (v. 1)
- Humble servant (vv. 3-8)
- Sacrificed His own life for us (v. 8)
- Highly exalted (v. 9)
- Name above all names (v. 10)
- Jesus Christ is Lord (v. 11)
- Glorious Father (v. 11)

Prayer Prompts

- Jesus, Your own humility has encouraged me because... (vv. 1, 7)
- Jesus, I bow my knee in worship and proclaim You as Lord over... (vv. 10-11)
- Thank You that because You took the form of a servant... (v. 7)
- Jesus, we praise You because Your name is... (v. 10)

RESPONSE – *Surrender to Him and His ways*

- I confess, Lord, my selfish ambition and vain conceit in… (v. 3)
- Jesus, instead of emptying myself like You, I tend to be full of myself when… (v. 7)

REQUESTS – *Ask the Spirit to guide prayer over concerns, resources, and relationships*

- Jesus, may the next generation embody Your servanthood by the way they… (v. 7)
- Help us as the Church to look to the interests of students so that… (v. 4)
- Jesus, because You emptied Yourself, empower the next generation to humbly serve __________ (*list areas of need in your community*). (vv. 7-8)
- Jesus, may You cause __________ (*name students who do not yet know the Lord*) to bow their knees and confess You as Lord! (vv. 10-11)

READINESS – *Encouragement and strength for spiritual battle*

- Jesus, because You have been given the name above all names, we can walk in victory over… (v. 10)
- Help the next generation exalt Jesus in their battle with… (v. 9)

A Generation Set Apart for God Prayer Guide

Daniel 1:1-20

REVERENCE – *Identify and celebrate God's praiseworthy attributes*

- He is the Lord over all earthly kings and rulers (v. 2)
- Giver of favor and compassion (v. 9)
- Rewarder of faithfulness (v. 15)
- Provider of learning, skill, and wisdom (vv. 17, 20)

Prayer Prompts

- God, You are Lord and king over... (v. 2)
- Lord, thank You for the favor and compassion You showed me when... (v. 9)
- I praise You for the wisdom You provided when I was facing... (v. 17)

RESPONSE – *Surrender to Him and His ways*

- Lord my King, I confess my lack of faithfulness in... (v. 12)
- I admit and forsake my temptation towards the worldly pleasures/comforts of... (v. 5)

REQUESTS – *Ask the Spirit to guide prayer over concerns, resources, and relationships*

- Lord, would You graciously set apart the next generation to... (vv. 6, 9)
- God, please show Your compassion to (*name a student*) so that they will... (v. 9)
- God my King, give learning, skill, and wisdom to the students at __________ (*name local college/university*) so that they will faithfully represent You by... (vv. 17-20)

READINESS – *Encouragement and strength for spiritual battle*

- Lord, give the next generation a resolve and zeal for holiness and devotion to You as they face... (v. 8)
- God, may Your favor bring victory over the enemy's attempt to __________ in the lives of the next generation. (v. 9)

ACKNOWLEDGEMENT

A book like this takes a small village. And since our Lord is magnified by thanksgiving (Ps. 69:30), we saw it most fitting to spill some ink to express our heartfelt gratitude to the many who made this project possible. Foremost and foundationally, we thank our Heavenly Father with our whole hearts for redeeming us and adopting us into His beautiful, diverse, and unified mutligeneration family. May this book reflect His heart to all generations!

Secondly, we are so grateful for our Strategic Renewal Staff and Board who faithfully support, prayer, and encourage one another. Specifically thank you to our board chair Jim Maxim who initiated the idea of creating a resource like this when he authored 21 Days of Breakthrough Prayer several years ago which ended up launching this multi-book series of 21 Day books to encourage and equip God's people in prayer. We are grateful for not only our staff contributors who authored several chapters (Daniel, Dennis, Len, Ricky, and Amber), but also for Carley Phelps who coordinated the layout and printing of this book serving once again as the "super glue" to hold all of the moving pieces together. Additionally, as an extension of our team, we're deeply thankful for Sara Romanov and her super power editing and proofreading skills. Also for Jay Phelps for his patient and creative graphic design expertise with the help of Ricky and Jordan.

Thirdly, we are immensely grateful for our partnering team of authors who are serving on the front lines of what God is doing in, amongst, and through this next generation. Thai and Angela Lam, Drew Humphrey, Katie Laitkep, and Paul Worcester, your faithful passion to raise up a generation of gospel-driven, glory-motivated, and Spirit-led men and women who lovingly obey the voice of our Good Shepherd to couragesouly follow and join Him in His mission to disciple the nations, is truly inspiring, convicting, and hope-filling.

Lastly, we are grateful for you reader, or should we say prayer, who has picked up this book with the intent to devote these next 21 days to seek God's face and trust His hand for the next generation. May you be engergized like never before to exalt Christ and fervently serve in Your role in discipling the next generation, beginning with prayer that leads to the fulfillment of our Father's purposes!

ABOUT THE AUTHORS

Daniel Henderson

President, Strategic Renewal and Global Director, The 6:4 Fellowship

As a senior pastor for nearly three decades, Daniel Henderson brought prayer-based revitalization to numerous churches. Now, as the President of Strategic Renewal and Global Director of The 6:4 Fellowship, Daniel is dedicating his full-time efforts to help congregations across the country and world experience renewal. Daniel is sought after for his expertise in leading corporate prayer. He has authored numerous books on biblical leadership and prayer, including *Old Paths, New Power* and *Transforming Prayer: How Everything Changes When You Seek God's Face.*

Dennis Henderson

National Director, The 6:4 Fellowship

Dennis Henderson left the senior pastorate after 54 years of pastoring to become the North America Director for The 6:4 Fellowship. He continues to consult with his home church, Northlake Church in Lago Vista, Texas, as the Pastor of Kingdom Advancement and Prayer. He and Billie have been married since 1965, and have four adult children and nine grandchildren. Billie and Dennis have a passion to help ministry couples and support the ministry of prayer in the local church through The 6:4 Fellowship.

Justin Jeppesen

National Director, The 6:3 Discipleship

Justin most recently served as a pastor and professor at the University of Northwestern in St. Paul, MN. He led hundreds of young adults, along with other staff, in the rhythms of prayer and the ministry of the word. Before serving in his role at Northwestern, Justin spent 10 years in pastoral ministry at a local church where he was first introduced to Strategic Renewal. He is a graduate of two coaching cohorts. Justin and his wife of 10 years, Maddy, have two kids and live in St. Paul, where they get to experience all the wonderful seasons God has created!

Len Crowley

International Director, The 6:4 Fellowship

Len Crowley is the Founder of *Forgiven Communities* – advocating for biblical church purpose and practice. He currently serves as the International Director of *The 6:4 Fellowship* and coordinates *6:4PRESS Publishing* and the *6:4 National Gathering.* During his nearly 40 years of Christian ministry, Len has been the lead pastor of four churches, a Bible teacher, a board member, and a ministry director. He also co-founded *Whole in One* (designing multi-ethnic collaborations), has led *PLI Global* (character-based leadership training), helped direct *Counsel & Capital* (a non-profit investment bank), and taught as a National Instructor with *Walk Thru the Bible.*

Ricky Cassford

Director of Communications

Ricky Cassford has been in ministry nearly his whole life. Growing up in the home of Salvation Army pastors, he has always enjoyed media, activities, and ministries that edify the Church. For the last 20 years, he has volunteered with his local church leadership to encourage spiritual growth within the church body through teaching, facilitating small groups, and worship, as well as writing, organizing, and performing dramatic presentations for special events and VBS/Day Camps. Ricky's heart beats strongly for men taking up "the mantle of Dad-hood" and intentionally pouring into their children. He is the author of the children's book *A Magnificent Treasure*, which captures a father's love for his daughter in a fun and fantastical way. Ricky currently lives in Lone Tree, CO with his beautiful wife, Heidi, and two of their four children..

Amber Doggett

Administrative Assistant, The 6:4 Fellowship

Amber started serving with Strategic Renewal in 2018. She left for a few years beginning in 2020, but not for long. While she was working as Dennis Henderon's assistant at Northlake Church, he became the National Director of The 6:4 Fellowship. She continued to assist him even through that transition, thereby rejoining the Strategic Renewal team in 2021, under the banner of The 6:4 Fellowship. She currently serves as the administrative assistant for 6:4, and feels tremendously blessed to serve pastors all around the world. Amber has been married to her best friend, Will, since 2008. Together they have 10-year-old boy/girl twins and a 4-year-old girl.

In 2022, in their Texas home, they felt the Lord lead them to leave and go on an adventure to the East Coast. They had no idea where they would end up, but after two months of searching, He led them to Moncks Corner, SC, where they currently live.

Thai Lam

Thai serves as Founder and Executive Director of the Revival is Family Foundation. Over the past 15+ years, he has given leadership to RIF CAMPUS, a campus prayer movement that is equipping college students to be praying leaders, and to COLLEGIATE DAY OF PRAYER, a movement that mobilizes the Body of Christ to unite in prayer for revival and spiritual awakening on college campuses. Thai has pioneered and led campus ministries at UC Berkeley, UCLA, Stanford, San Jose State, KU, and UMKC. He came to faith in Jesus as a freshman at UC Berkeley, graduated with a degree in Religious Studies, and then studied Cross-Cultural Missions at Fuller Seminary.

Angela Lam

Angela serves on the leadership team for the Revival is Family Foundation. She has been in leadership with RIF CAMPUS, equipping college students to be praying leaders. Angela has served as a short-term missionary to Argentina, China, Guatemala, Hong Kong, India, Malaysia, Mexico, Namibia, and Panama and has been on staff with various missions organizations, including Teen Mania Ministries, NewGenerations International, and Harvest Evangelism. She attended William Jessup University, where she studied Management & Ethics and Biblical Theology, and she also completed the Impact School of Ministry in San Jose, CA.

Drew Humphrey

Drew began serving as College Mobilizer in 2024 and has been serving on ministry staff at Highland Baptist Church in Waco, Texas, since 2009. For the past decade, he has served as the College Pastor at Highland, and he continues in this role alongside working part time for the SBTC. Drew and his wife Holly both grew up as pastor's kids and met at Baylor during college. Now, they parent four children together and love ministering through their local church. Drew graduated from Baylor University in 2013 with a Bachelor of Arts in Biblical Studies and received his graduate degree from Dallas Baptist University in 2017 with a Master of Arts in Christian Education.

Katie Laitkep

Katie Laitkep was working as a hospital teacher when God called her to join *Revive Our Hearts* as a staff writer. She serves remotely from Houston, Texas, where God sustains her through saltwater beaches, Scripture, and her local church. Her weekly newsletter, "On the Horizon," encourages readers to live in light of the reality that today we're one day closer to being home with Jesus.

Paul Worcester

Paul Worcester serves as the National Collegiate Director for the North American Mission Board, where he focuses on encouraging, inspiring, and equipping collegiate leaders in 900+ college ministries across North America. At NAMB, he pioneered an interactive coaching network that involves hundreds of leaders each year. He spends his days traveling to campuses leading trainings on evangelism, disciple-making, and missions. Paul is the founder of several ministries, including Christian Challenge at California State University, Chico which he led for many years, seeing a movement of God with over 1,000 college students making professions of faith during his time there. Recently, his family moved to the North Shore of Oahu, where they help invest in young leaders at Good Soil Discipleship School when he is at home. Paul also founded Campus Multiplication Network, an international and interdenominational coaching and resource ministry impacting leaders in many nations. He is a co-host of three podcasts, including the GenSend Podcast with Shane Pruitt and Lacey Villasenor. He has authored several books for collegiate leaders and students including: *5 Leadership Principles For Collegiate Ministry*, *The Fuel & the Flame: Ignite Your Life & Your Campus for Jesus Christ* and *Thrive: Cultivating A Faith That Endures* with LifeWay. Paul has degrees from the University of Oklahoma and Southeastern Baptist Theological Seminary. His wife, Christy, is his dearest partner in life and co-laborer in ministry, and they have two kids and an adorable French bulldog named Ollie. When he is not working, you can find him surfing or skateboarding with his kids or taking Ollie to go search for some crabs on the beach.